'ARRY'S 'OLIDAY; B'LOGNE AND BACK.

PHIL MAY

Yours sincerely Phil May

PHIL MAY

The Artist & His Wit

DAVID CUPPLEDITCH

LONDON · FORTUNE PRESS

CHARLES SKILTON PUBLISHING GROUP

For Sylvia

*The captioned cartoons, unless otherwise stated,
originally appeared in "Punch"*

ISBN 0 284 98593 7

© David Cuppleditch, 1981

Made and printed in Great Britain by
Anchor Press Ltd, Tiptree, Essex
from typesetting and layout by
Alacrity Phototypesetters,
Banwell Castle, Weston-super-Mare

Published by THE FORTUNE PRESS
(Charles Skilton Publishing Group)
115 Old Street London EC1

CONTENTS

*A typical Phil May pose,
using the chairback to rest
his sketch-pad upon*

Phil May in 1894

*Phil May and his dog,
"Mr Blathers"*

*A cartoon of Phil May
by "Spy"*

Foreword by Miles Kington

In the *Punch* offices at 23 Tudor Street there is a room which still houses the old *Punch* round table around which generations of artists and writers have talked, eaten and sometimes drunk too much. On one wall of that room there hang two large frames containing all the photographs of all the members of the table, past and present. The twentieth-century members crowd into one frame, looking sometimes quizzical, sometimes assured, but all different from each other. In the earlier frame the Victorian members look all much the same: bearded, comfortable, a bit plump and satisfied, all rather middle-aged. With one startling exception. In the bottom row a clean-cut face stares out at you, almost fiercely commanding your attention. No matter who it was you went to look at, that was the face you end up looking at — Phil May, a hawk among the Victorian chickens, a modern man staring into the twentieth century while his colleagues are content to let the old order go on as long as it likes.

During my twelve years at *Punch* I have often wandered into the room just to look at May's face and wish that, of all the people on the wall, I could be privileged to meet him. Not that I would know what to say if I did. I have spent an even larger part of that twelve years talking to most of the cartoonists of today and one thing I know is that whatever else they talk about, cartooning is not high on their list. Money, yes — especially if it is being earned by other cartoonists, for they are a competitive lot — nibs, ink, Vermeer, pubs, football, but not the art of cartooning unless practised by someone safely dead. And of all the cartoonists they talk about from the past, Phil May is the one that comes up most often.

It's easy to see why. Almost single-handed he made it possible for the modern cartoonist to operate. Victorian cartoons were furnished almost as heavily as Victorian rooms were, with details which are the delight of a social historian but hard work for the eye. Phil May threw out the clutter and overnight left room for the line to move and the eye to breathe. More than that, he made the *artist* the master of the cartoon. Before him, there was always a feeling that the cartoonist was illustrating a literary idea — very often, indeed, I believe that nineteenth-century artists simply drew up the visual version of an idea fed to them. After Phil May, it was impossible for the artist ever again to feel an inferior version of the writer (if they still do, it is on the trivial grounds that they are often rotten spellers).

As if this wasn't enough, cartoonists often feel that Phil May was one of them because he was the first to establish a reputation as a drinking man's cartoonist. Why I do not know, but *Punch* writers tend to be loners and cartoonists tend to be gregarious, flocking to the pub together and even, God help us, going on holiday together in droves, and staying out very late at night. An anthology of cartoonists' escapades would make a hair-raising volume. That the first modern cartoonist should be the first highly convivial cartoonist is almost too much to hope for.

Yet, however high his reputation stands, it is curious how little is known about him, outside his drawing, and you will find otherwise well-read people who swear blind that Phil May was an Australian, or even that he carved his initials underneath the *Punch* table. He was a man about whom myths sprang up and facts did not. Every time I stared at that proud and daunting face in the *Punch* table room, I wished there were some book which would tell me the truth and the whole truth about him. Now, thanks to David Cuppleditch, there is. All modern artists should be grateful, but from me he gets a special vote of thanks.

Mr Punch: "WALK UP, WALK UP, LADIES AND GENTLEMEN! JUST A-GOING TO BEGIN!"

8

1 Early Days

N A BRISK spring morning in 1864, when the mist strayed over the dales and mingled with the smog of Leeds, Sarah Jane May produced her seventh child. The baby, a small frail boy, was born on April 22nd in a neatly kept two-up-two-down Georgian terrace house in the suburbs of Leeds. She named the child Philip William May after his father, but right from the start he was known simply as Phil.

Sarah's husband, a failed businessman and eternal optimist, had just started on a new venture as a commercial traveller, and the future looked relatively bright. But the strain of many disappointments showed on Sarah's face. Her life now was a far cry from the days of her courtship in Newcastle, where she had met her future husband for the first time. Philip May Senior had been sent by his father to serve an apprenticeship under the celebrated engineer George Stephenson, but despite this good start he did not have a successful career. As Phil May admitted later in life, "My father was very unlucky. He started a brass foundry business, but his partner cleared off with all the brass. His engineer consulting business was not much better." The family fortunes had been dissipated by the time of Phil's birth and Philip's new job, a Godsend at the time, was the last straw.

Young Phil May's early struggles were severe. In 1873, when he was nine years old, his father was killed in a riding accident. At this time Phil had been at school for only a year, though a certain promise had already been detected in the boy by a Mr Howgate, a local art dealer and gallery owner. "Phil May," he later recalled, "a mere toddler, was often brought into my Leeds gallery by his father or mother. I was particularly struck by the youngster's keen interest in the pictures, his innumerable questions and shrewd comments. In return for my help and advice he presented me with a coloured drawing signed 'Phil May aged nine years'; the drawing was strangely prophetic because it depicted Punch" (and it now hangs in the Leeds Municipal Collection).

Yorkshire in the 1870s was a hard, cold county; Leeds was especially bad, having suffered the upheaval of industrialisation. It was a place for work and its children were brought up to be seen and not heard. There were few toys in the May household — "Ther' wasn't the money t' go round" — and the children were left to devise their own amusements. Phil and his elder brother Charles would lounge about the back streets of Leeds, living more in their imaginations than in the real world. Theirs was a grim environment of shabby cobbled streets and gas lamps, but at home they could always rely on a hot meal from their mother's stewpot.

Phil's first ambition, soon thwarted by his family, was to become a jockey. Perhaps his love of horses was inherited from his father, who, his son was later to recall, "was singularly clever, as an amateur, in drawing horses, and not less fond of riding them." Phil's second love was the theatre, and he took great delight in dressing up: a paper hat could easily become a crown, or a discarded curtain a royal cloak, while dull Hanover Terrace or Kendal Lane could be transformed by imagination into Buckingham Palace — or deepest Africa. The fertile imagination

Phil May's parents
Sarah Jane May   Philip May, Sr.

Phil May's aunt,
Mrs Robert Honnor, who
was remarried when
this photo was taken

Charles May,
Phil's older brother.
An early pencil
drawing by Phil May

which was to prove so immensely useful in later life was already being kindled.

During many long, lonely evenings the three May boys, Charles, Phil and the youngest brother, Bert, would gather round their mother to hear tales of their aunt who lived in London. She was married to Bob Honnor, lessee of the famous Sadlers Wells Theatre. And she was an *actress* — an actress of considerable repute who played the star role in *Black Eyed Susan*, a play produced under her husband's management. She also played Oliver to her husband's Fagin in *Oliver Twist*, also produced at Sadlers Wells about this time. George Cruikshank designed the sets for this latter play from his original illustrations to Charles Dickens' novel.

During the 'forties Sarah had stayed with her sister in London and been introduced to London society. Not only had she met Cruikshank and Samuel Phelps, but also Charles Dickens himself, who had presented the Honnors with an autographed set of his books. As Sarah recalled these memories the boys listened, enthralled. Though the names meant little to Phil, the drawings of Cruikshank fascinated him. As her children grew sleepy, Sarah would sing to them: she had a good voice, Phil later remembered, and her renditions of "The Irish Emigrant" and "Kathleen Mavourneen" stuck in his memory.

Thinking back to these early days, it was Augustus Moore, the brother of George Moore, who recorded that, "Phil May was a delicate little fellow, and was made a butt of by the other boys, a victim of many practical jokes." However, in the thick of this rough and tumble he soon discovered his own way of rebuffing his tormentors: he learnt the hard way that if he made them laugh they would leave him alone. He soon learnt to accept his own poor physical attributes and to rely instead on the charm and guile of his personality. With his intelligence and sense of humour he could easily outwit the heaviest of pig-sticking bullies.

Phil's schooling was sparse and erratic, yet what little he got was well used. He attended St George's School from 1872 to 1875, Oxford Place School from 1876 to 1877, and spent a few months at Park Lane Boarding School in 1877. A contemporary from those days remembered his being quite good at art and winning a T-square and drawing board as prizes. It was not uncommon for children in those days to be educated in a very intermittent fashion, Sunday Schools being left to attempt to fill the gaps. Phil himself was sent to the St George's Church Sunday School where he was lucky enough to have as his teacher Richard Ainley, who had a passion for amateur theatricals. Ainley was in fact an excellent raconteur and entertainer — while his son Henry was to become the darling of the Edwardian stage — and his enthusiasm greatly impressed his young pupil. Plays and music-halls were at this time all the vogue, and so yet another budding hopeful joined the queue for theatrical recognition.

When St George's Sunday School entertained the Good Templars Lodge, Phil May had his first chance to deliver a public recitation. His "Little Jim" was wildly applauded: the reception brought a grin to the young lad's face and gave him the idea of organising a troupe. With four or five boys from Miss Smith's school in Woodhouse Lane he founded the Hero Club, reserving for himself the offices of president, secretary and treasurer. In these capacities he personally designed a banner and generously inaugurated the society by giving a glorious tea party — appreciation of which was somewhat dampened when its members learnt that they had paid for their feast with their own subscriptions, collected by Phil in his capacity as treasurer.

The aim of the Hero Club was to entertain, and the members built a toy theatre for just this purpose. Phil provided the scenery and more elaborate characters, while props were produced by others of his ingenious little friends. A tin sheet was used to give an extremely realistic simulation of thunder, while a humming top could sound just like the distant tones of a cathedral organ. Another clever contrivance was the arrangement of a series of glass screens to give a creditable representation of "Pepper's Ghost". These various experiments were all tried out on immediate relatives who, much to the club members' amazement, enthusiastically applauded and even clamoured for an encore.

Phil May's zest for life was not dampened when he left school and started his first job as a barrister's clerk in the office of Mr Percy Middleton. A fellow clerk under Mr Tindal Atkinson recalled this new experience:

> There were about half a dozen barristers congregated in Pease's Building, South Parade, in very uncommodious chambers and their young clerks used to assemble together in their absence and indulge in noisy pranks, of which I'm afraid even the youngest and liveliest of barristers would have seriously disapproved. Phil May was always up to larks, and how he ever drifted into the post of barrister's clerk I cannot imagine. Nothing could have kept him chained to the law. He made caricatures of all the barristers, hankered after the stage, and very quickly disappeared from legal chambers.

His next job, in an estate agent's office, was just as unsuccessful: he spilt ink all over a set of plans and left hurriedly, never to be seen again. Down on his luck, he dusted pianos in Archibald Ramsden's music store for half a crown a week, until being appointed time-keeper in an iron foundry — from which job he was soon discharged for refusing to dock anyone for being late (if, that is, he was on time himself). For a lesser man this unhappy succession of failures might have promised ill, though in Phil May's case it merely meant that the right job was yet to be found that would fit his talents.

Eventually salvation appeared in the form of the son of Fred Fox, the scenic painter. Phil had befriended him, and it was he who suggested that Phil should set his sights on the Grand Theatre which had just opened in Leeds, and where Fred Fox was in charge of the backcloths. "It was about this time", Phil May later recalled, "that my artistic career began." Engaged on the humble task of helping to mix the distemper, he nevertheless enjoyed himself thoroughly right from the start: it was the first job in which he felt at home, and he could later happily reminisce:

> Young Fox and some other boys called Ford, Sammy Stead and I used to rehearse pantomimes. Our stage was a back street, and our scenery was designed with a stick in the gutter, but we omitted nothing. The star-traps were all marked out, and we made our descents by flinging ourselves on our faces in the muddy road. I was always a sprite, and carried the "Book of Fate" which had a prominent place in all our productions.

He was in his element, strutting about the stage, helping wherever possible. Sometimes he would be called upon to sketch costumes for the wardrobe room or to suggest suitable masks for the make-up department. He became friendly with most of the actors who starred at the Grand and would sometimes be commissioned to draw their portraits at a shilling a sketch. After a time he became quite a dab hand at likenesses and as his skill increased his prices rose from one shilling to five. Some of these drawings were exhibited in the theatre foyer, and caused much comment.

As his remuneration grew, so did Phil's independence, and he was able to leave home to share lodgings with three or four of the other boys from the theatre at five shillings a week. Having become a master of lightning sketches, he now began to

THE SERVANT QUESTION

"Oh, I say, 'ave you seen the Papers about 'Shall we do without Servants?' I should like to see 'em try, that's all!"

"Yus, and me too!"

HOW THE POOR LIVE

The Rev Mr Smirk has brought an American millionaire friend to see for himself the distressed state of the poor of his parish.

(He'll give them a little notice next time.)

A NEW GAME

Playing at Jubilees; or, Making a Knight of it

A STORY WITHOUT WORDS

"A GREAT OPPORTUNITY"

CORONATION ROBES A SPECIALITY.

attempt, with growing confidence, full-length portraits three feet high. One interesting example is "The Vital Spark", a portrait of Jennie Hill which can be seen in the Leeds collection, though this colour picture measures only 18½ by 10½ inches. The head is well drawn and a natural aptitude for line and composition is shown which is quite remarkable in the work of a fourteen-year-old lad.

Perhaps it was these drawings in the theatre foyer which brought Phil May to the attention of the editor of a small local comic journal, *The Yorkshire Gossip*. He was engaged to draw for them on a weekly basis, thereby supplementing his income from the Grand. Unfortunately, the fly-by-night journal died as suddenly as it was born, disappearing after only four weeks, its most notable future claim to fame being that it was the first publication to carry Phil May's work.

One highlight of Phil's early working life in Leeds was the occasion of a procession through the centre of the city. As it was an occasion on which his diminutive stature placed him at a distinct disadvantage, he had the bright idea of settling himself in a window on the first floor of Queen Anne's Buildings in New Briggate, but in his ecitement to get a still better view, he leaned over a little too far, overbalanced and fell from the window on to the tall hat of a gentleman below, ending up with his legs stradding the unfortunate man's neck. Assisting his victim to his feet, Phil apologised "for coming upon him so suddenly", but also thanked him for breaking his fall. The surprised gentleman, who suffered nothing worse than an abraded nose, from contact with the rim of his hat, gallantly accepted the apology.

In 1880 Fred Stimpson, who had a travelling burlesque company, commissioned Phil May to play the small parts and, in addition, to complete six sketches a week to be used as posters advertising the show. The pay totted up to the princely sum of twelve shillings and sixpence a week and Phil was delighted with his change of fortune. He made his professional acting debut at the Spa Theatre in Scarborough, playing such parts as Simon Tappertit in *Barnaby Rudge*, François in *Richelieu* and the cat in *Dick Whittington*. It is not difficult to imagine his excitement: completely stage-struck, he promptly went off to have himself photographed as Mephistopheles, Tony Lumpkin and "A Swell". No doubt he considered that these photographs would be useful to use as postcards when the great day arrived and Phil May, actor-extraordinaire, would be asked to take the star rôle in a West End theatrical extravaganza.

Phil's ability to act convincingly was evidenced in a prank. An old friend of the family who collected birds' eggs complained to him that, although he was most anxious to buy some rare eggs from the man who lived opposite him, the neighbour would not part with them. A plot was laid: a party was thrown and the owner of the eggs was invited. As the guests assembled, a mysterious Japanese prince was introduced to the circle. Curiously, the conversation turned to birds' eggs, and the prince asked to see the neighbour's notable collection. "Certainly, your Royal Highness," he replied, trotting off to return with his hoard. The prince picked out the eggs for which his friend yearned, and offered to buy them. "No, no," insisted the neighbour, "please take them with my compliments; it would be an honour!" Shortly after the departure of the prince, Phil May arrived, expressing keen disappointment that he had not seen the royal visitor!

Now, in his new acting venture, Phil's wildest dreams were beginning to come true, and he would strut about the stage rendering Shakespeare in the manner of his idol Henry Irving. He had always loved dressing up and now that his aspirations were taking shape he began to imagine himself as Mark Antony, King Lear or

Early caricature of
J. L. Toole, in watercolour

Jenny Hill, an early
watercolour, in the Leeds
City Art Gallery

Watercolour study of
costume design for the
Grand Theatre, Leeds

Phil May at 16   *Lilian May, Phil's wife*

Othello. Unfortunately, as yet the only rôles which came his way were Bottom, Puck or one of the Three Witches. In fact, Phil May's image of himself was grossly mistaken: Stimpson's only reason for keeping him on was as a source of cheap advertising.

Late in 1882 Phil was back in Leeds, where he designed the dresses for the Christmas pantomime at the Grand Theatre. Fred Storey fell ill during the last fortnight of the run and so Phil was allowed to stand in for him, but as a general dogsbody about the theatre he was becoming restless. As Augustus Moore put it, "He was sickened with the hand to mouth existence he had led since he was a boy."

However, one development of that Christmas of 1882 was to be of lasting significance. There was a young woman in Phil's audience who was much impressed by his performance. She ran a confectionery shop just opposite the theatre. Young, energetic and pretty, she had previously been married to Charles Farrer. She had noticed the cheerful odd-ball actor already, buying cigars from her little shop, but had never spoken to him. To him it was a source of great surprise that any woman should be attracted by his peculiar features. This was Lilian.

Meeting Lilian was to change Phil May's life. She was a little older than him and the stigma of having been married before had left her few friends. Phil, however, was not one to worry about narrow middle-class values: he strolled into her shop and bowled her over. She was fascinated by his unconventional life-style which, compared to her own stifled existence, seemed gloriously romantic and carefree. She longed for the same freedom but her innate matter-of-factness and common sense tied her to the shop.

They began to meet frequently. Phil's visits would brighten Lilian's whole day: sometimes he would act the fool, sometimes just amuse her with amazing tales. In a

16

SHAKESPEARE ILLUSTRATED

"I HAVE YET ROOM FOR SIX SCOTCHES MORE."

Antony and Cleopatra, Act IV, Sc. 1.

SHAKESPEARE UP TO DATE

"YOU SHALL NEVER TAKE HER WITHOUT ANSWER, UNLESS YOU TAKE HER WITHOUT HER TONGUE."

As You Like It, Act IV, Sc. 1.

QUITE OF HER OPINION

Gushing Young Woman (to famous Actor): "OH, DO YOU KNOW, MR STARLEIGH, I'M SIMPLY *MAD* TO GO ON THE STAGE!"

Famous Actor: "YES, I SHOULD THINK YOU *WOULD* BE, MY DEAR YOUNG LADY!"

AMENITIES OF THE PROFESSION

Rising Young Dramatist: "SAW YOUR WIFE IN FRONT LAST NIGHT. WHAT DID SHE THINK OF MY NEW COMEDY?"

Brother Playwright: "OH, I THINK SHE LIKED IT. SHE TOLD ME SHE HAD A GOOD LAUGH."

Rising Young Dramatist: "AH — ER — WHEN WAS THAT?"

Brother Playwright: "DURING THE ENTR'ACTE. ONE OF THE ATTENDANTS DROPPED AN ICE DOWN HER NEIGHBOUR'S NECK!"

short space of time their friendship warmed to courtship, and courtship to love. It placed a new responsibility on Phil's shoulders; he needed to consider his financial affairs. If he married Lilian, how could they live? Like a touring actor, he began to look towards London for his answer. London was the Great Metropolis where topsy-turvy adventures occurred every minute, where fortunes were made over night and reputations hung in the balance — where Fleet Street was the hub of it all, neatly laundering the city's gossip for the Victorian press.

It was clear to Phil that he must now give up his rôle of penniless actor, gypsy artist and joker-extraordinaire if he was not to be a drain on Lilian's slim resources. The onus lay on him to evolve as a responsible human being. Just what exactly to do was a difficult decision for the young idealist, but one which now had to be faced if he were ever to think seriously about marrying Lilian.

Armed with determination and a great sense of purpose, he spread his wings for London with a sovereign in his pocket. As Augustus Moore drily commented, "Fifteen shillings and fivepence halfpenny bought him a third class ticket, and vanity and temptation cost him four shillings and sixpence at the Gaiety Bar." But as Phil May himself recalled, "What did it all matter? I was in London — the lap of luxury." His first port of call was the house of his actress aunt, who was now remarried to another actor, Fred Moreton. Unfortunately she was not exactly pleased to see him at her door in a street in Islington. Remembering that her father, Phil's grandfather, had brought the family into disrepute through his impetuosity, she feared that her nephew — already infamous in family circles — was following suit. Phil's maternal grandfather had been quite a success on the stage and, after graduating from Dublin University, he had been disinherited by his father for refusing to join the priesthood. He had married his leading lady at the Dublin theatre and the zenith of his career had come in Drury Lane, when he received Napoleon III and the Empress Eugénie on the occasion of their state visit. This hankering after the stage had, his aunt noted, been passed from grandfather to grandson.

Nevertheless, a worried Mrs Moreton took Phil in, fed him and gave him a bed. The next day his new uncle showed him the sights of London and paid his fare back to Leeds. Equally determined, Phil got off at the first stop and walked back to London. Then, to quote James Thorpe, "he fell upon hard times and touched the nadir of his ill-fortune". For no good reason, he landed up in Clapham. He had nowhere to stay now that he had exhausted the option of his aunt, and so, despite the fact that it was winter, he was reduced to sleeping on park benches, on the Embankment, or in carts at Covent Garden. He begged for broken biscuits outside public-houses and quenched his thirst at free fountains. Later recalling these days for an interviewer from the *Idler*, he said: "I don't know whether painful early experiences are in vogue just now with the people you interview, but in my case the experience was real — painfully so."

Phil was not physically strong and this period of his life took its toll in later years. However, in other ways there was something to gain from it and he learnt much about the hypocrisy of life from rubbing shoulders with the tramps and reprobates of London. He realised how artificial was the moralistic cant of Victorian High Church vicars, when all around them lay the depressed, rejected and unhelped working-classes. This hypocrisy of London society grated fearfully against his sensitivity till even Leeds began to seem idyllic in comparison. Alcohol was the only means of escape for the downtrodden drop-outs of London, and even that generated its own despair. Phil May himself touched bottom but would not give up: his determination and stubbornness, his sheer obstinacy, kept him going.

Old Lady: "No, thanks. I don't want any for the garden today."
Boy: "Well, then, can we sing yer some Christmas Carols instead?"

THE OPTIMISTS

There's always something to be thankful for

"Well, anyhow, I'm glad we ain't got nuffin on that'll spoil!"

Pantomime Child (to admiring friend): "Yus, and there's another hadvantage in bein' a hactress. You get yer fortygraphs took for noffink!"

"What d'yer call the new baby, Aurelia?"
"Peace!"

"OH, GEORGE DEAR, THE LANDLORD HAS RAISED THE RENT!"
"HAS HE? *I* CAN'T!"

Mr Grumble: "I SEE BY THE PAPER THAT MOUNT VESUVIUS IS IN ERUPTION."
Mrs G.: "OH, I'M *SO* GLAD!"
Mr G.: "THERE YOU ARE AGAIN, MARIA. NOW WHY ON EARTH SHOULD YOU BE GLAD?"
Mrs G.: "WELL, YOU CAN'T BLAME *ME* FOR IT, THAT'S ALL!"

INDIRECT ORATION

"OH, IF YOU PLEASE, MUM, THERE'S NO MEAT FOR DINNER. THE BUTCHER 'AS BEEN AND GONE AND NEVER COME THIS MORNING!"

At night under the stars he would think of Lilian, and her faith in his ability gave him something to fight for, though he had parted with his walking-stick in exchange for a bacon sandwich on Westminster Bridge, and his clothes hung in tatters. However, he was very near to packing it all in, when he met the proprietor of a photographic shop near Charing Cross. After seeing some of his drawings, this benign Pickwickian character befriended the threadbare young lad and published one of them in postcard form. The sketch was a caricature of Irving, Toole and Bancroft. Although it was produced under a partnership arrangement, the unfortunate publisher lost about £5 on the venture. However, it was a start for Phil May: there was a glimmer of light at the end of his tunnel and, although his shopkeeper friend was hardly prosperous, he would often take him to a restaurant near the old Pavilion for a dinner of beef *à la mode*. "It was damn' good!" recalled Phil with some profundity. Through this same relationship he was introduced to an actor by the name of Rising who played at the comedy theatre. Rising was in turn a great pal of Lionel Brough, and through him Phil was eventually introduced to the well-known and much respected doyen of the Victorian theatre. Brough was impressed with the caricature of his three rivals and bought the original sketch from the shopkeeper for two guineas. On the strength of his meeting with Phil, Brough gave him letters of introduction to the editor of the weekly newspaper *Society*. It was a stroke of luck for May, who might not hitherto have considered himself a candidate for letters of introduction, especially not from so distinguished a gentleman as Lionel Brough. Besides which, he had found himself a backer. Much of Victorian society and business was based on personal recommendation — then even more than now it was a case of who you knew, not what you knew.

Although his drawings now began to appear in *Society*, there were still periods when Phil May suffered penury and would gladly have taken up his chalks and drawn on the pavement. At last, however, a drawing of Bancroft in *Society* so impressed Edward Russell of the Haymarket Theatre that he gave Phil an introduction to the editor of a new journal, the *St Stephen's Review*. Filled with expectation, Phil hurried along to meet the great man but was told that he was busy and that the journal in any case had enough cartoons to last it several months. Desperately disappointed, Phil left a few drawings with the old man at the door and slouched off down the street, his head hung low.

The summer of '83 had come and gone; it was winter once again and he had lost two stones. He looked terrible and, worse than that, was deeply depressed. The long months of privation were wearing his body away, and still he was no nearer success in financial terms than when he had first arrived in London ten months before. Nothing was left to him but to return to Leeds under a dismal cloud of failure. At least he could see Lilian again, though he dreaded having to explain his lack of success. As he boarded the Leeds train at King's Cross he was filled with remorse. Even the cold, damp night reflected his gloom.

His fears about returning home were at least unfounded: the welcome he received was heartwarming. His mother promptly packed him off to bed and nursed him back to health. Within a week he was back on his feet and anxious to see Lilian. He ordered a new suit for the occasion, wrapped up a bouquet of flowers and marched down to the confectionery shop. Lilian was delighted to see him: the intervening months had passed slowly. Although she noticed the tell-tale marks of struggle on his person, she said nothing. They saw a great deal of each other over the next two weeks and Phil learnt to smile once again. Then, out of the blue, a telegram arrived: "EDITOR ST STEPHEN'S REVIEW REQUESTS MEETING URGENTLY — EDWARD RUSSELL".

2   Romano's and The Press

WILLIAM ALLISON, the editor of the *St Stephen's Review*, had been let down by his regular cartoonist over a double-page drawing for the Christmas edition. A new artist who had been commissioned had failed miserably and so Allison was looking for a replacement, but there was little time. Allison's business manager, Edeveain, showed him a selection of sketches, which included a few by Phil May which immediately caught his eye. "This lad looks promising," he said hopefully.
hopefully.

But where was Phil May? Edeveain quickly contacted various business associates, including Edward Russell of the Haymarket theatre, who was able to tell him that Phil had returned to Leeds, and who managed to winkle his address out of the photograph shop proprietor. Russell immediately sent Phil May a telegram. As soon as Phil received it he set off for London. As he walked into Allison's office he must have been unaware of the impression he gave, but Allison recorded many years later:

> He was a lean, cadaverous looking youth with close-cropped, very dark hair, and eyes that looked through you like gimlets. If ever there was the fire of genius in any eyes, it was there in Phil May's and whatever mistakes I have made in my life, I made none that time, for I knew right off that I had found something quite abnormally excellent.

Allison explained his situation to Phil. Could he deputise? He most certainly could — Phil leapt at the chance. In order to complete the commission, Phil rented a small hotel room near the Princess's Theatre, where he could work in peace. After the work had been completed and paid for, he stayed on until all the money had been spent. Frugal measures were essential — such as 'going out for breakfast and dinner', which meant walking the streets during hotel mealtimes. Eventually the hotel manager uncovered this ploy, but, happily, instead of insisting that Phil leave the hotel, he allowed him to stay on until his finances improved.

Phil hoped that, if he remained close at hand, further commissions would follow after the publication of his four full-page drawings and centre-spread cartoon entitled "The Coming Paradise" which appeared in the Christmas number of the *St Stephen's Review* in 1883. But nothing came up. Lionel Brough, however, came to his aid once again and introduced him to Charles Alias, the costumier, who engaged Phil to help design costumes for a forthcoming production of *Nell Gwynne*.

Charles Alias was the son of a French village surgeon, who had been cut off with the proverbial shilling because he had refused to follow his father's profession. He had arrived in London in the early 'seventies — penniless like Phil May, so he could still understand what it was like. His first job had been wardrobe assistant of the Philharmonic in Islington, but through avid learning and diligent saving, he set up a business in Soho Square in a house that had once been a convent. By 1883 Alias had established a prosperous costumier's business in St Martin's Lane.

Phil May obviously remembered this time in his life, and Alias in particular, with affection because the small, dapper figure of Charles Alias appeared in many

"The Bar of the House"
(At Romano's)
by Phil May

From left to right in this fantasy are
Labouchere, Gladstone, Romano,
John Corlett, The Shifter, The
Brown Mouse, Arthur Roberts (as
the Speaker), Edgar Lee, Parnell,
Jack Percival and Chippy Norton

of his later theatrical illustrations: he is easily recognised by his dark-tinted pince-nez and black hair brushed straight back.

Unfortunately the play, *Nell Gwynne*, which starred Florence St John, Arthur Roberts and Lionel Brough, enjoyed only mediocre reviews and was soon forgotten. However, there were consolations. Alias introduced Phil May to Romano's and he was immediately captivated by its atmosphere of Falstaffian good fellowship and playful exuberance, which suited him far better than the aesthetic conversations which oozed from the decadence of the Café Royal. The two highly bohemian journalists, William Wilde and Augustus Moore, were far more in their natural element at Romano's than would have been their famous brothers, Oscar Wilde and George Moore.

One morning when it was bucketing down with rain Phil May had to deliver some sketches to Alias on foot. He arrived soaked to the skin. Alias, who took pity on him, told him to take off his sodden clothes. He lent Phil a pair of Turkish slippers and a quilted Regency dressing gown and took the dripping clothes into one of his work rooms to dry out by a stove. He had to go out to see some customers but left Phil with pencils and paper, asking him to work on some designs in the cosily heated office. He would have ample time to finish them before Alias returned to take him to lunch.

Alias kept his appointments and on his way back to the office popped into Romano's for his usual aperitif. Standing at the other end of the bar, wearing a

French gendarme's shako, a brigand's cloak many sizes too big and tall Hessian boots, and surrounded by a laughing crowd of friends, was Phil May.

"Are my clothes dry yet?" inquired Phil innocently.

Amusing incidents such as this seem to have cemented the friendship between Alias and May and although "The Juvenile Shakespeare", a book on which they collaborated, came to nothing, Alias went on to produce, with Phil's aid, some of Augustus Harris's most spectacular costumes.

During this time both Alias and Phil May were often to be found in Romano's, as was William Allison who frequently lunched there. The offices of the *St Stephen's Review* were in John Street, Adelphi, very close to Romano's. Started on March 17th 1883, the *St Stephen's Review* was independently financed and expensively produced. With less than £500 as collateral and production costs of £150 a week, there was little room for error. Allison, however, was the right man for the job: his solid background of Yorkshire, Rugby, Balliol and the Bar helped him on the way to becoming a successful entrepreneur. He was quick to see the potential in the formula adopted by the American magazine *Puck*, with its political cartoons in colour and in March 1884 remodelled the *St Stephen's Review* along these lines, with a greater emphasis on the pictorial. For this purpose he engaged two cartoonists, Tom Merry and Phil May: Merry's well-worked, somewhat wooden cartoons contrasted heavily against May's sensitive line but it was a good combination and the two artists shared a mutual respect for each other. Merry, the elder of the two, and already very popular, usually took up a "two-pager" with his large-scale political cartoons. His panache soon began to rub off on to the less experienced Phil May.

With fresh confidence and high hopes Phil now returned to Leeds and proposed to Lilian on the strength of this staff appointment. She accepted, and they were married just before Phil's twentieth birthday. Lilian sold the confectionery shop in Briggate and they moved into rooms in Covent Garden. Their possessions were few, yet they were extremely happy. Lilian enjoyed the hustle and bustle of London life, though it was not quite the sort of social melée she had expected.

Phil worked enthusiastically for his new employer and supplemented his meagre income with further contributions to the *Penny Illustrated* and *Pictorial World*. From this time on his drawings managed to express a great vivacity and sense of enjoyment. He was beginning to establish himself as a regular contributor to the London press, and his portrait caricatures were starting to be noticed.

In personal terms, there is no doubt that Phil was a popular member of the *St Stephen's Review* staff, mixing well with everyone. Edgar Lee Tasker, Allison's sub-editor, took Phil along to the Savage Club, where he met many of his boyhood idols, such as Bancroft and Toole, in person. Sometimes Merry would accompany them to the Savage, but he rarely visited Romano's: the infamous crowd who frequented this fashionable retreat were too bohemian for Merry's tastes. There were "The Shifter" and "Gubbins" from the *Sporting Times* and "The Roman" himself, who played host to the reprobate band of Victorians who used this cheerful meeting place as their club. Romano, who was of Italian extraction, was simply an opportunist whose main wish was to earn as much money as he could in as short a space of time as possible.

Fleet Street men could choose their local haunts from a variety of pubs providing a convivial atmosphere in which they could talk business or simply drown their sorrows. Romano's was just one of many, but it was the one where Phil May was first introduced to London society. Is it any wonder that he modelled his lifestyle on

Workman (*politely to old Lady, who has accidentally got into a Smoking Compartment*): "YOU DON'T OBJECT TO MY PIPE, I 'OPE, MUM?"
Old Lady: "YES, I DO OBJECT VERY STRONGLY!"
Workman: "OH! THEN OUT YOU GET!"

Swell: "MIND MY HORSE, BOY, AND I'LL GIVE YOU TWOPENCE."
Boy: "I WILL, IF YOU'LL MIND THE BABY!"

Gent (*rushing out of club in a terrific hurry*): "I SAY, CABBY, DRIVE AS FAST AS YOU CAN WATERLOO— LEATHERHEAD!"
Cabby: "'ERE, I SAY, NOT SO MUCH OF YOUR LEATHER'ED, IF YOU PLEASE!"
[*Goes off grumbling.*

NOTES OF TRAVEL

Foreign Husband (*whose Wife is going to remain longer*): "GIF ME TWO TICKETS, VON FOR ME TO COME BACK, AND VON FOR MY VIFE NOT TO COME BACK!"

Alfonso Nicolino Romano

Romano's bedecked for the Royal Wedding of 1893

Romano's Advertisement Card with Learned Quotations by The Shifter

its careless extravagance? He found much pleasure in its smoke-filled rooms, where he would hold court with open-handed generosity. For him it was a forum where the rich and famous rubbed shoulders with the inconsequential, and where whisky blurred the distinction between the two. It was also a haunt of Gaiety Girls and their admirers, "the crutch and toothpick brigade", and there was much flirting over champagne. Perhaps it was the charms of the chorus girls who frequently supped at Romano's, or The Roman's free and easy attitude towards credit, that attracted such throngs of stage celebrities and sportsmen.

Romano had started out as a waiter at the Café Royal, opening his own doors in the 'seventies with the idea of running a bar along the lines of a French café. On his first day he went into the City and managed to get three bottles of champagne on credit from three different firms, with which to start business. He later made a point of trusting his own customers, whose accounts, in the early days, were patiently chalked up for weeks on end. On one occasion when a fire broke out, certain old habitués arrived on the scene and directed the firemen to hose the chalk from the slates on which their particular accounts were kept. Nevertheless, Romano continued to be lenient with good clients and it was rumoured that, at the outbreak of the Boer War, he was owed many thousands of pounds by "men about town".

Before long the cooking at Romano's became excellent and the restaurant a great success. Although it was shaped like a rifle gallery, Romano's was a congenial rendezvous with its red velvet cushions and neat tablecloths.

Romano's restaurant witnessed many lively scenes, as on the occasion when a vivacious group of young officers dropped open umbrellas from the gallery on to those supping below. One diner who resented this rude descent of parachutes decided to teach the officers a lesson when they came downstairs, but, as the young men were more handy with their fists than had been expected, he came off badly. Edward VII, when Prince of Wales, used to visit Romano's occasionally and once sent a telegram regretting his inability to attend a dinner there. The restaurant was still in being for several decades after Romano himself died early in the present century, though its great days were over.

In his time Romano had entertained some bizarre characters. He certainly saw the seamy side of life as well as the flamboyant, and his patience must have been tried at times by impecunious patrons. One of these was Stephen Coleman, known to all Bohemia as "Fatty". His twenty-four stone required a special chair in the Pelican Club; his past was a mystery — in confidential mood he would darkly hint of an Army career. He roamed from club to club, hotel to hotel, restaurant to restaurant; he was vaguely assumed to be "connected with the management". But Fatty rather overdid things and towards the end even the most tolerant of his friends began to shrink from the inevitable request for a fiver; his list of "useful" friends grew short.

It was during this dark period of his existence that Fatty, sitting in his usual corner at Romano's, saw Phil May enter in the company of a wealthy cigar merchant. Fatty grasped the situation in a twinkling. He knew that Phil would be obliged to leave shortly, and so greeted him effusively — so effusively that an introduction to the wealthy cigar merchant was unavoidable. After a while Phil left the bar to keep an appointment, but not before he had slipped his rich companion a warning about Fatty's financial weaknesses.

The next morning Fatty appeared at Phil May's flat. "I'm glad I caught you," he said, "it's my dear wife's birthday and I haven't any money to take her out, but I know as an old friend you'll lend me a fiver."

Record of the famous fight
between Phil May & Fatty Coleman

"I'm very sorry, Fatty, I haven't got a penny on me," Phil replied. Fatty lost his temper. Phil reeled back in bewilderment. "Look, I haven't got any money," he repeated, "but I can give you an order to take to my florist." So off Fatty sauntered to Bond Street.

Some time later Phil met the cigar merchant in Romano's and was received with notable coldness. "What's the matter?" he asked. "What have I done?"

"Done!" replied the plutocrat, "you've done nothing except the best turn you could possibly have done me when you introduced me to Fatty."

Then the cigar merchant related his story. "After you left us the other night I remembered it was my wife's birthday the next day and, knowing there was no-one in London who could order a dinner like Fatty, I gave him carte blanche to order the best dinner for a dozen of my friends at the Café Royal. I got a few of my pals together and the dinner was perfect. But what touched me to the heart was the present which Fatty brought for my wife — a magnificent spray of flowers." Phil looked astounded but kept listening.

"Did any of my rich guests think of her? Not on your life! But poor old Fatty, broke as he is, and against whom you warned me — yes, *warned me*, was a courteous gentleman, and I shall never forget his delicacy, his ... his ... dammit, yes, *sweetness*! Well, I had a couple of boxes at the Empire and when the dinner was over I managed to get hold of Fatty. 'Look here,' I said, 'you and I and the wife will go into one box and the rest can have the other — I'd like the three of us to be together.'"

The merchant went on: "And with tears in his eyes — absolutely with tears in his eyes, poor old Fatty said it was impossible. I asked him why, and he told me that the bailiffs had just gone into his flat and had upset his own wife. He didn't know who to turn to because all his old friends were dead. 'But they're not,' I told him. 'I'm your pal tonight. What d'you owe?' I asked him and he replied, 'A year's rent, a paltry £150.' 'Is that all?' I said, and hauled out my cheque book and gave him a cheque for £200. I can show a little gratitude to a noble-hearted fellow when that noble-hearted fellow is down on his luck."

Knowing that Fatty's "flat" was a furnished bed-sit in Pimlico and that his own bouquet was behind the successful ploy, Phil May nevertheless also knew that if he gave Fatty away he would simply gain the tobacco magnate as an enemy for life; he decided to say nothing. Eventually a growing antagonism between Fatty and Phil May actually reached the point of physical violence, occasioning their famous fight, an event recorded in a drawing by May, which contrasts Fatty Coleman's obesity with his own frail frame.

Phil May was always a sensitive man, and particularly generous with money. Allison, on the other hand, had a quick eye for profit. When he began to publish a series of cartoons based on the "Rake's Progress" in the *St Stephen's Review* and realised how popular they were proving, he halted production of the magazine and sold them separately at thirty shillings a set. Readers of the *St Stephen's Review* had to settle for a bowdlerised cartoon instead. This piece of business acumen brought him in a comfortable £750. In this series the cartoonist Merry had depicted Gladstone as the Rake. Phil May was prompted by this idea to caricature Gladstone as the gravedigger in his "Old Gravedigger's Christmas Eve", published on December 27th 1884. In the graveyard were shown the tombs of many well-known men killed in Egypt — implying prophetically that the new grave being dug was for Gordon, who was then holding out at Khartoum. The cartoon, chillingly lit by moonlight, had a gruesome air and created quite a sensation.

Surprisingly, however, Phil May's style did not immediately catch on with the public, much to the astonishment of Allison, who considered May the best artist on his staff. Merry's work, on the other hand, was extremely popular, despite its defiencies — and even Allison had to admit that Merry's drawings were crude. "People used to ask me why I allowed such 'vulgar' cartoons to be published,' he was later to comment, going on to explain: 'I meant the cartoons for the public and not for fastidious critics of the paper.'" It was not an unreasonable attitude considering he needed every penny he could get in those precarious early days. It was, in short, sensationalism, and Allison's rôle as a patron of the arts had to take second place to his position as a successful editor, and Merry's popularity helped to push the sales of the *St Stephen's Review* up to seven thousand copies a week.

In retrospect Allison was to comment about the early part of 1885: "All was going well with the paper now. Our finances were still weak, but we flourished exceedingly nevertheless, and political excitement was growing higher as the attempted relief of Gordon hung fire." During the second week of February 1885 came the news of Gordon's death. It was a Wednesday morning and Phil May immediately dashed off a sketch of Gladstone as Macbeth and Gordon as Banquo's ghost, which astounded the newspaper world by appearing in the *St Stephen's Review* the following morning, beating them all off the stocks. In those days it was a slow process to reproduce a drawing — how had May's cartoon been dealt with so quickly? Part of the secret was his use of transfer paper instead of ordinary drawing

Minister's Wife: "TOMMY CROWTHER, YOU HAVEN'T WASHED YOUR FACE TODAY!"
Tommy Crowther: "'TAIN'T SUNDAY!"

MISUNDERSTOOD

Mild Old Gentleman rescues a bun which Child has dropped in the mud.
Child (all aglow with righteous indignation): "THAT'S MY BUN!"

"THAT NEW BOY'S A BAD BOY, TEACHER. HE SMOKES!"
"NO, I DON'T SMOKE *NOW*, TEACHER. I USED TO!"

"WHAT ARE YOU DOING IN THAT CUPBOARD, CYRIL?"
"HUSH, AUNTIE! I'M PRETENDING TO BE A THIEF!"

paper, which facilitated the quick transfer of drawing to printing block. This was the first of his experiments with transfer paper. First attempted simply to save time, his later developments of the technique were to be more adventurous.

Allison had entered Fleet Street as the newspaper boom was just beginning: there was a rapidly growing demand for news and discussions of current affairs. Perhaps the most successful of his fellow newcomers was George Newnes who started *Tit-Bits* in 1881. As a prize in one of his many competitions Newnes offered a job on the staff of *Tit-Bits*. The winner was Cyril Arthur Pearson who was later to become manager of the paper. Pearson resigned in 1890 to start his own *Pearson's Weekly*, while Newnes himself first published the *Strand Magazine* in 1891. Alfred Harmsworth was a contributor to *Tit-Bits*, and he started *Answers to Correspondents* in 1888. These three great pioneers of Fleet Street were to shape the future of newspaper publishing. Newnes was the least committed member of the trio — although he acquired the *Westminster Gazette* and founded *Country Life*, he later gave up publishing to become a Member of Parliament, and he was eventually knighted. Pearson won an excellent reputation for *Pearson's Weekly* and later established *The Daily Express* and bought the *Evening Standard* and a number of provincial newspapers. However, his career was tragically cut short when he lost his sight. Refusing to regard blindness as a hopeless handicap, he joined the council of the National Institute for the Blind and devoted much of his time and energy to founding St Dunstan's.

The third member of this group — the most dynamic and certainly the most autocratic — Alfred Harmsworth, had had no doubts about his career when he became a freelance journalist at the age of sixteen. When he started *Answers to Correspondents* at the age of twenty-three he was suffering from indifferent health, and operating from a tiny office in Paternoster Row (at a rent of 12/6d a week) he fought desperately to keep both himself and the small weekly alive. Within a year he had pushed the circulation of his journal to a million copies. With the aid of gimmickry, and the help of his brother Harold, he also successfully launched *Comic Cuts*, *Home Chat*, *The Sunday Companion* and *The Union Jack*. His success was so rapid that he was able to buy the *Evening News* and found the *Daily Mail* only eight years after launching *Answers*. Harmsworth was once described as "a ceaseless Napoleon of Fleet Street" and, it was said, if you hadn't been sacked by him you weren't worth knowing. In addition to capturing the newspaper market he also produced educational publications such as *The Harmsworth History of the World* and *The Harmsworth Encyclopaedia*. All these enterprises laid the foundations of his Amalgamated Press.

A third cartoonist, Matt Morgan, joined the *St Stephen's Review* in 1885. He shared the double-page spread with Merry, alternating with him week by week. Morgan, a seasoned campaigner, had worked for *The Illustrated London News* and *The Illustrated Times* and had made his reputation on the radical paper *Tomahawk*, where his sharp satirical wit earned him both antagonists and admirers in abundance. He was one of the most popular Victorian caricaturists. Eventually he emigrated to the United States and painted panoramas of the American Civil War. As part of the Merry-May team he was a useful asset to the *St Stephen's Review* and was after a time to replace Merry altogether.

During the autumn of 1885 a Mr W. H. Traill of the Sydney *Bulletin* arrived in London, looking for a cartoonist to work for him in Australia. The job was advertised at £15 a week, with a guaranteed three-year contract. Traill was much

AN UNPOPULAR IDOL!

How Billy and his Sunday-schoolmates intend to wreak their vengeance, if only a snow-storm be propitious, on the Embankment some Sunday afternoon about Christmas time!

"Poor little Dickey Birds! Dear little Dickey Birds!"

MUCH ADO

"Mamma-a-a! We're crying! Tum up 'tairs an' see what's de matter wiv us!"

impressed by one of Phil May's cartoons, "The Welsher" (published during Derby week, it depicted Gladstone being pursued by an infuriated Opposition and British Bulldog). On the strength of this piece of work he offered May the job, but May was in no hurry to give up his newly acquired stability and turned it down. Traill proposed doubling the salary to £30 a week, however, and this tipped the balance. It far outweighed the £10 he was getting from the *St Stephen's Review* and, besides, there was his health to consider. May decided that the trip would do both him and Lilian good: a sea voyage in itself would be a tonic. Allison tried in vain to dissuade him: Phil's mind had been made up.

The news of his decision to go to Australia soon reached Romano's, and a crowd of well-wishers gathered to see him off. The departing Phil stood champagne all round (he himself drank whisky) and there were emotional scenes as the time came for the final handshakes. Among the party was an impecunious old actor who wrung the artist's thin fingers with both his wrinkled palms, apparently overcome by the tragic significance of the moment. "Phil, old man," he was finally able to stutter, "lend me half-a-crown, will you?" When May eventually returned to England and rejoined his old friends at Romano's, standing at the bar he once again found the old actor, wrinkled, shaky and bleary-eyed. He was the first to welcome the wanderer home: showing no surprise, and no particular pleasure, he wrung his hand as before and begged: "Phil, old man, lend me half-a-crown, will you?"

As a going-away present to Phil May, Allison organised, in the ground floor and three upper rooms of the *St Stephen's Review* premises, an exhibition of May's work. It was to last two days and would bring May a little extra spending money; the press were invited so as to generate as much public interest as possible. Allison considered this the least he could do for the cartoonist who had helped him build up the popularity of his paper, though he was still regretting May's departure. Allison saw a new stubborn streak in Phil: although he was ready to admit that 'There was no place like London to get good work appreciated' he was nevertheless prepared to gamble his future in Australia, where he could easily be soon forgotten by his London public. Phil May was, however, confident in his future and on November 11th 1885 he and Lilian set sail for Sydney.

Old Jones: "YES, MY BOY, *THERE'S* WINE FOR YOU, EH? I BOUGHT TEN POUNDS WORTH OF IT THE OTHER DAY!"
Brown: "WHAT A *LOT* YOU MUST HAVE GOT!"

3   *The Period in Australia*

HE VOYAGE to Australia was a well-earned break for Phil May. He and Lilian waved good-bye to one or two friends at the quayside, and could then simply relax. However, the artist's hand could never be idle for long. One of their going-away presents was *The Orient Guide*, the blank pages of which were soon covered with sketches of fellow passengers, while the backs of maps soon bore kindly caricatures of members of the crew, inscribed "To Lily May, December 1885". A Leeds collector was lucky enough to pick up this copy of *The Orient Guide* from a market stall for sixpence in 1932 and among the many delightful sketches found a brilliant self-portrait of May among its pages; it was even possible to follow the stages of the Mays' journey from drawings. Early ones were of fellow passengers while later Australian squatters appeared, and at the end was an unfinished drawing of a well-known Australian politician. How the book found its way on to a barrow in Leeds was of course a mystery, though it seems that at one time it belonged to Philip Bradley, a good friend of May, who owned a warehouse in Leeds: his signature appears on the first page and elsewhere in the book.

When May left the *St Stephen's Review* he was replaced by the Edinburgh-born cartoonist George Halkett, who took up May's preoccupation with caricaturing Gladstone. Eventually these drawings appeared in book form under the titles *New Gleanings from Gladstone*, *Gladstone Almanack* and *The Irish Green Book* (the last concentrating on the Home Rule debates of 1887). Halkett, however, could not replace May in the eyes of Allison. Neither his work nor his personality inspired the same rapport with Phil May's Yorkshire compatriot: Phil's relationship with Allison had been based on mutual admiration.

However, thoughts of Fleet Street were far from Phil May's mind as he relaxed on deck, swathed in a rug and sipping cocoa liberally laced with whisky. He was more concerned about his coming reception in Sydney and whether he and Lilian would like Australia. He need not have been concerned about his reception: it was heartwarming. Traill was at the quayside to greet them and gave them a foretaste of the wonderful hospitality they were to receive in Australia.

For the next three years May worked strenuously and exclusively for the *Bulletin*. His talent was soon recognised and appreciated, while both he and Lilian made many friends in Sydney. They first found down-town rooms on the corner of Pitt Street and Bathurst Street, later moving to a hotel on the corner of Hunter Street and Castlereagh Street as they grew wealthier. May produced some nine hundred drawings during his time on the *Bulletin*, and the personal impression he made on those he met was recalled by A. G. Stephens in a tribute to May: "Wherever was his studio, there the door was open to all good companions. He befriended many; injured none. Never was he heard to say an ill word, or known to do an ill turn. Cheerful, careless, he seemed the best of Bohemians and the happiest of artists. No one could be more sincerely loved." May's motto, said Stephens, was "'Draw firm! Be jolly!' ... It was 'Draw, Phil, or die!' May lived by his art, not for it. Often

Studies & Sketches Abroad

A REMINISCENCE OF AUSTRALIA

Bush Magistrate (to Visiting Magistrates who have had a wild night): "LOOK HERE, FELLERS, BEFURE WE GO ON WID THIS CASE, WHERE THE DEVIL DID YA GIT TO WHIN OI MISSED YA LAST NOIGHT?"

JOHN CHINAMAN IN SYDNEY.

OVERHEARD IN SYDNEY, N.S.W.

"WELL, YOUNG SCAPEGRACE, ARE YOU GOING BACK HOME TO LET YOUR PEOPLE KILL THE FATTED CALF?"
"OH, YOU DON'T KNOW MY GOVERNOR, *HE'S* NOT THAT SORT; HE'D MORE LIKELY KILL THE BALLY PRODIGAL."

A Lost Leader

The Minstrel

The Mongolian Octopus—His Grip on Australia

his dinner must have depended upon his talent for catching a likeness. He was in the position of a dog forced to beg for a biscuit. May got the biscuit."

This view of May's art sounds a little unfair, but then May was a failed actor turned artist, who was uncertain about his future. Even Traill felt uneasy about his appointment, wondering what his readers would think of the effortless ease which appeared in May's work. Pointing out the work of the other *Bulletin* cartoonist, Livingstone Hopkins, Traill suggested to Phil: "Couldn't you finish up your drawings a bit — more like this."

May's reply was characteristic: "When I can leave out half the lines I now use I shall want six times the money."

In fact May was setting a precedent. Most of the staff of the *Bulletin*, such as "Jules Francois" Archibald, a master journalist, and William Macleod, were Australian by birth; only Phil May and Livingstone "Hop" Hopkins were imports. Hopkins was an American and, like Phil, was helping to fill in the gap of indigenous comic artists. The collection of individualists which made up the *Bulletin* staff were to mould it into one of the most rampant, free and radical papers of the century. By the turn of the century, according to the New Zealand cartoonist David Low, "The *Bulletin* had grown a team of social and political artists it would have been hard to beat anywhere in the world. In the matter of style and ability in draughtsmanship, that was good; in the matter of satirical approach and content it was better."

The *Bulletin* damned the crimson bonds of Empire and all its hypocrisy. It was strictly an Australian paper for Australians and its caricaturists found in its pages a new freedom to vent their caustic wit. Phil May's cartoon of John Bull as the Angel of Deliverance hovering over a possible colony with a Bible in one hand and a bottle of rum in the other, typified its spirit. It was not only in Sydney that the *Bulletin* found a large readership: it even became known as "the Bushman's Bible" and boasted admirers from Alice Springs to Perth.

David Low, who joined the paper in 1911, by which time some of its rough edges had been worn smooth, said of Phil May's time: "Hundreds of imitators jumped to the disastrous conclusion that the way to make drawings was 'to dash them off' like Phil May, who laboured so successfully to eliminate the appearance of effort." It was during his three years in Sydney that May perfected this trick of elimination. "Perhaps I should say the printing machines of the Sydney *Bulletin* were my real master," he once confessed. Shades of Linley Sambourne appeared in his work and there was a touch of W. G. Baxter's Ally Sloper in his humour, but his approach was original.

In an interview with the *Sketch* Phil May described his method of building up a drawing:

> First of all I get the general idea, of which I sketch a rough outline, and from this general idea I never depart. Then I make several studies from the model in the poses which the drawing requires, and redraw my figures from these studies. The next step is to draw the picture completely, carefully putting in every line necessary to fulness of detail: and the last to select the particular lines that are essential to the effect I want to produce, and take all the others out.

In some cases he transferred his figures from sketch book to working page with tracing paper. He nearly always worked with a very sharp pencil or crayon edge so as to achieve simple, strong lines. George Halkett, May's successor on the *St Stephen's Review* later wrote:

> The one important lesson learned from his *Bulletin* work was the value of a longer and heavier line, made imperative by the large scale of his cartoons. With this enforced

practice, May's actual facility of hand was increased, and some of the productions of this time are remarkable for their breadth and decorative sense. New South Wales politics gave him an excellent chance, and May found a ready audience for his wild spirits in black-and-white. His series of "Things we See when we are out without our Gun" touched the Colonial sense of humour, and the inventor became the hero of artistic circles in Sydney.

Phil May in turn enjoyed the novelty of Australia and was pleased of an assured income, while the opportunities of meeting other artists were a source of stimulation. There was a constant stream of visitors to the May household in Sydney, including the painters Charles Conder and John Longstaff. Lilian enjoyed entertaining Phil's guests and fellow-journalists in the relaxed atmosphere of the hotel. The Australian weather was also proving kind to Phil May, whose health slowly improved in the southern sunshine. There were frequent social events to look forward to in addition to visits by friends; on one occasion when the Mays went to see *Faust* at the Melbourne Opera a strange thing happened:

> The leading tenor was unable to appear, but at the last moment the manager with difficulty persuaded a well-known local singer to take his place. In spite of his inexperience on the stage, his excellent voice and the circumstances of his appearance won the complete sympathy and applause of the audience and he scored a tremendous success. The excitement, however, was too great a strain on a weak heart, and on one of his exits through a trapdoor he dropped dead. The dramatic group, lit from the hole in the stage above, with the pallid figure of the triumphant singer surrounded by angels and other characters of the opera in costume, the distant excited cheering of the audience, unconscious of the grim happening, all produced such a deep impression on Phil May that he made a quick sketch of the scene, which he afterwards developed into a painting.

In the busy social whirl of Sydney, Lilian had not really noticed just how much Phil was beginning to drink: secretly he had come to rely on the effects of alcohol and, as time went by, his dependence on it was to increase. In the Colonial web of pink gins and bonhomie it was easy not to pay too much attention to his excesses. Later in an interview with the *Idler* Phil admitted to one of his binges:

> Take one example, the happy husband going home late in the morning, stealthily walking upstairs, lest he should wake his wife, and has just removed his coat and one boot when his wife suddenly wakes. "What are you doing?" the wife exclaims. "Oh, it's all right," the husband replies nervously as he readjusts his boot; "I've got to get up early this morning, my dear," and forfeiting his rest, goes down to breakfast. Well, that's not fiction. It actually happened — in Australia. I was the culprit!

 One of May's drinking companions was another expatriate, Blamire Young, who had arrived in Sydney in 1885. Twenty-three years old and an idealist, he had gone to Australia in search of "Colonial experience". Young and May found they had much in common: both were Yorkshiremen, and they shared an insatiable appetite for art. Unlike May, however, Young was a classics scholar and brilliant mathematician (he had accepted a post as mathematics master at Katoomba College, New South Wales) and was, in addition, six foot three in height and a born athlete. He must have looked like a giant beside May, and yet May was an enormous influence on Young. On the subject of art the two found no difficulty in seeing eye-to-eye: they were certainly in agreement on the point that Whistler was the greatest of living artists. Blamire Young has been largely forgotten today, though he enjoyed an excellent reputation during the early years of this century

Songs
and
Their
Singers

From a
series
in *Punch*

Carol Singers:
"OH, REST YOU, MERRY GENTLEMAN,
MAY NOTHING YOU DISMAY!"

when prints of many of his paintings reached a wide audience. Like Montague Dawson, he won the popular acclaim of the press, but after going out of fashion has never made a comeback.

Phil May met Young after his contract with the *Bulletin* had expired. He had decided to remain in Australia for a few months more and to take up painting — for which purpose he was looking for a quiet studio in which to work. Young's studio was the ideal hideaway. It had been built in the grounds of Katoomba College in 1887 and was well equipped, if somewhat bizarre: the floor was strewn with a couple of fine Mizapore rugs and a Persian carpet, the stone fireplace had a blue tiled insert and the chimney breast was ornamented with a broad band of purple; from the ceiling hung four scarlet wrought-iron lamps while the windows at one end of the room were curtained with Madras muslin and at the other with floral chintz. In a corner niche was a specially made wooden settee, painted scarlet, and covered with a gold plush cushion. To complete the studio were a few rush-seated chairs, one or two drapes and the usual essential paraphernalia.

Phil May arranged to share the studio with Young, and made frequent use of it, in return for the privilege of which he tutored Young. As J. F. Bruce explained:

> Soon a little coterie of artists and amateurs including Godfrey Rivers and Mr Theodore Fink, frequented the studio where Phil May, then in the enjoyment of his greatest fame and powers, genially played the rôle of presiding genius. At that time he was greatly enamoured of the new French style, using large brushes with the "square touch". In this manner he painted a few portraits, and also whimsically decorated the four panels of the door with portraits of his host, himself, Theodore Fink and Godfrey Rivers. In the gilt ground of each panel ran its appropriate legend: "Art is long" (Young); "My stay is short" (May); and "A Fink of beauty is a joy for Rivers".

Unfortunately this artistic *jeu d'esprit* was destroyed when the studio burned down shortly afterwards. However, Young himself stayed on at Katoomba until 1893, when he returned to England.

May was later to realise that he was not suited to painting, despite the tipsy encouragement of Conder and the respect of Jack Longstaff. It was draughtsmanship that was his strong point; as A. G. Stephens wrote:

> May's art was essentially athletic. Herkomer meant this when he said that May's line was like the stroke of Joachim's bow. A good drawing by May is a "tour de force". What his eye clearly saw, his hand accurately expressed, in so far as a black-on-white line can express objects. The mechanics of the feat, the correspondence between aim and realisation, are so absolute that one receives the pleasure like that given by a wonderful stroke at billiards, or a clean somersault in the circus. There is in May's drawings an intellectual beauty of precision and harmony that is the basis of their artistic merit. Many inferior draughtsmen have become memorable artists. May, lacking his draughtsmanship, would have counted for little. One prizes him chiefly because he could give to a line individual power, particular charm.

Phil May's unbounded enthusiasm, as well as his talent, had always impressed his friends, and one in particular, Theodore Fink — an amateur artist with a healthy bank balance — saw in May the glitter of genius. Knowing his own limitations as an artist and realising that no amount of money was going to buy him talent, he decided instead to invest where talent already lay. He suggested that a spell in Rome and Paris would benefit May as an artist, giving him the opportunity to study old masters and new techniques and so perhaps gain a fresh approach. He generously offered to pay the expenses of both Phil and Lilian: it was an offer which

Phil May could not afford to refuse, for, as James Thorpe commented, "In those days living was extravagant in Sydney, and May's earnings did not provide much surplus over the weekly expenses." However, in a way Fink's generosity was misplaced: he sought to encourage Phil May as a painter, but Phil himself came more and more to realise that his true form of expression was in black and white. He once said to a friend:

> I can never understand how it is *everyone* can't draw. It is so simple. You only need to start with a straight line. I part my hair in the middle. So should everybody. But, in the case of those who don't, just imagine it parted. Then draw a straight line from that hair parting to the middle of a man's heels. Then you have your straight line — everything else is a curve. It's quite simple.

Although he was not to make a painter of Phil May, Theodore Fink's great generosity was enormously appreciated by the Mays. Fink made £1000 available to them (a considerable sum in those days) and they sailed out of Sydney harbour in the autumn of 1888, destined for Europe. It was just what they needed.

Old Lady (giving a very diminutive nip of Whisky to her Gardener):
"THERE, DENNIS, THAT WHISKY IS TWENTY YEARS OLD!"
Dennis: "IS IT THAT, MARM? SURE, 'TIS MIGHTY SMALL FOR ITS AGE!"

Funiculì Funiculà

Late for Mass

4 Return to Europe

NAPLES was the port where the Mays left the boat to complete the rest of their journey by train. Glimpsing the famous Bay of Naples and sketching the urchins on the quayside, Phil thought it looked pretty much like many other cities in the world. From its squalid, smelly port to its grandiose colonnades and façades he remained unimpressed. Rome was a different matter: he immediately responded to its sense of ancient and romantic heritage. As he was later to write to his brother, "Be it ever so crumbly, there's no place like Rome." They saw the great sights — the Colosseum, the Sistine Chapel — and revelled in the exhilarating new freedom of travel. It would have been easy to spend their whole allowance on sight-seeing, but Phil May was determined to justify his patron's generosity. Most evenings Phil would drink himself silly at the trattorias, but during the day he studiously copied Old Masters, dutifully sending examples of his work back to Fink. At the same time he continued his association with the Sydney *Bulletin* and regularly supplied them with drawings. May also wrote to his old friend Allison, saying that, on his return to England, he would very much like to draw for the *St Stephen's Review* again. Allison was delighted

William Allison
Editor of the "St Stephen's Review"

Colonel North
"The Nitrate King"

and immediately wrote back; he had heard of the reputation May had established for himself in Australia, and asked him to send some sketches. The year 1888 was drawing to a close, and instead of replying to Allison's letter Phil decided to surprise him with a flying visit. Leaving Lilian in Rome, he made his way overland to Calais, travelling to London on the boat-train, where Allison takes up the story:

> It so happened that Colonel North was going to give a tremendous fancy-dress ball at the Metropole Hotel on January 4th 1889. It occurred to me that it would be really great to have Phil May at Colonel North's ball, and I wrote to the Colonel asking him if he would stand the expense of bringing Phil May over from Rome. He asked what it would cost, and I replied that about £50 would do it, which was little enough in all conscience, but Colonel North did not agree. I received his answer at the Junior Carlton Club, where he was surrounded by friends such as Randolph Churchill and Lord Abergavenny. So I went back to my office, where to my surprise and delight I found Phil May sitting in a comfortable armchair. This was splendid, for I soon got him an invitation to the ball and he did a brilliant double-page drawing of the whole affair.

When Colonel North saw the cartoon in the *St Stephen's Review* he tore it up in wrath and kicked out the old canvasser who came to ask how many copies he would like. What specially enraged him was the sketch of him as Henry VIII, saying: "Cost me £8000 and I can't get a drink!" (Which was true: the unfortunate Colonel had not been able to get a glass of champagne at the evening end.) However, when his fury had subsided and North had reconsidered May's fine piece of work he began to see its funny side; he went out and bought a thousand copies of the paper to distribute to his friends. Upon reflection it seemed clear that the "can't get a drink" caption applied only to himself and *not* to his guests.

By this time Phil May was on his way back to Rome, where he and Lilian remained some months. When their funds had been noticeably depleted they moved to Paris, where, at that time, lived many English and Americans. Initially May shared a small studio with William Rothenstein in the rue Ravignan. For a rent of four hundred francs a year, it was sparsely furnished with a camp bed, wooden table and cheap stove, to which poor comforts Rothenstein had, however, added two beautiful Louis XVI chairs and fine Liberty draperies. Phil made little use of the studio. "His failing was already noticeable," Rothenstein noted later, "and the influence of Conder, who shared it, was detrimental to regular work." To the student artists he met, Phil May appeared a man of wealth who could afford all the models he needed. He and Lilian had an apartment at Puteaux; Conder and Jack Longstaff, whom Phil had met up with, were then living in Montmartre.

After a short time May left Rothenstein to team up with Harry Thompson, a Gallicised English landscape painter who had a fine studio and garden in Puteaux. Jack Longstaff (who at the time was struggling to keep a roof over his head, though he was later to become a distinguished portrait painter) said of this period:

> In Paris I was a frequent visitor to Phil May's house at Puteaux. At this stage of Phil May's career, I think some of his best work was done. He particularly delighted in getting us all together in his studio, when the evening would be devoted to music, and he would afterwards insist on putting us up. In the morning the studio would look like a battlefield. Phil was intensely musical, and had one of the sweetest tenor voices I have ever heard. It was about this time he displayed a strong desire to become a painter. So one evening I took him to an art class to enrol him as a student, he having provided himself with a liberal amount of material in the shape of drawing-blocks, pencils, charcoals, etc. His ardour seemed to lessen very rapidly after our arrival, and after making a few drawings from the model we withdrew to a neighbouring café where we

Scrumble: "Been to see the Old Masters?"
Stippleton (who has married money): "No. Fact is"—
    (sotto voce)—"I've got quite enough on my
hands with the old Missus!"

Scrumble: "So sorry I've none of my work to show
    you. Fact is, I've just sent all my pictures to the
    Academy."
Mrs Macmillions: "What a pity! I did so much want
    to see them. How soon do you expect them
    back?"

SENDING-IN DAY AT THE ROYAL ACADEMY

"But it is impossible for you to see the President.
    What do you want to see him for?"
"I want to show him exactly where I want my
    picture hung."

Little Guttersnipe (who is getting quite used to posing):
    "Will you want me ter tike my bun down?"

*The artist in this cartoon is
Harry Thompson, May's Paris friend*

Courtyard of the Hôtel de France,
Montreuil

A sketch in Picardy

discussed his prospects as a painter pure and simple, and he finally left full of schemes for painting pictures. But never again did he attend the class, nor did I ever hear him make any reference to the matter. It was his first and last visit to an art school. I believe Phil May could have become a good painter — but he fortunately recognised where his great strength lay, and confined himself to black and white. Phil and I spent much time together in the streets and on the boulevards, and a favourite haunt was the Café de Paris where he found types of every nationality. After each visit his sketch-book would be filled with notes and sketches of the people he had seen.

It was in the back streets that May's inspiration lay. He produced a series called "Life in Paris", a set of priceless gems which are among his very best work. Like many other of his friends, Harry Thompson appeared in some of Phil May's work, a compliment which Thompson returned by inviting the Mays to some of his "Octaves" — dinners of eight courses for eight people at eight o'clock — which both Phil and Lilian enjoyed immensely.

Phil and Lilian would go on sketching outings, too. On one occasion Lilian packed a luncheon basket and Phil's sketching materials and they set off for their picnic in the country and presently arrived at a small village. It was a fine day, so they stopped for a drink at the local café and glanced at the menu. It looked so appetising that they ignored their basket and ate at the café instead. As so often happens during pleasant and relaxed lunches, the afternoon quickly disappeared. On their way home they were confronted by the *Octroi*. The "town duty" official demanded to see the contents of their basket, then insisted that they pay duty on the chicken. They were staggered, but no pleas of innocence would shift the bureaucratic stalwart in his demands: "You weel 'aff to pay juty on your chicken, Monsieur."

"Pay be damned!" answered Phil, and they sat at the roadside and consumed their bird. The bewildered official looked on in amazement — there was nothing in his little book of rules to cover such a situation. Having finished, Phil and Lilian departed, graciously handing him their wishbone, upside down.

Among the drawings which Phil May sent to Allison in the autumn of 1889 was a set of ink sketches called "The Parson and the Painter", based on an Australian curate whom the Mays had met in Sydney. It proved a popular theme. However, it was Phil May's double-page cartoon entitled "Crime" which took pride of place in the Christmas issue of the *St Stephen's Review* that year. Phil May took up "The Parson and the Painter" idea when he and Lilian returned to England in the Spring of 1890, when Allison suggested that he should improve it: it was turned into a series of autobiographical notes featuring Allison as the parson and May as the painter. The result was a series of incidents concerning the Rev. Joseph Slapkins, an unsophisticated parson, and his artist nephew Charlie Summers, who together visited well-known theatres and clubs in London and journeyed as far afield as Whitby and Scarborough, and even Boulogne and Paris.

Allison was thoroughly conversant with the world of racing, being an authority on horse breeding (he later wrote *The British Thoroughbred Horse*), and though Phil May knew little of such technicalities he loved riding and frequently attended race meetings. Once, during an interview with the *Idler*, he was questioned about his attitude towards betting. He strongly denied any connection with gambling — he knew Lilian would read the article and, anyway, he did not wish to be known as a gambling man. In spite of the denial, he had won large sums of money at "Bush" race meetings in Australia. "I believe that some people imagine that I am a dare-devil sporting man," he said during the interview. "I don't so much mind the

application of the first part of the phrase, but I am not a betting man, and have never been to a race meeting in my life, except on the one or two occasions when I went on behalf of a paper."

May looked old when he was young, yet remained young when he was older — a boy in spite of his wrinkles. "If I had a son," he said, "I would not like him to go through the struggle that I have had." But Phil and Lilian never did have any children. In the early part of 1890 they moved to 34 King Street, Covent Garden and settled down to their old routine, Phil continuing to draw for the *St Stephen's Review*. In July of that year, however, the paper ran into trouble. After a series of court cases over the next two years concerning take-over bids and various bits of nastiness and skulduggery, the paper was left in a weak state. Eventually it succumbed to the power struggle, dying officially on September 8th 1892. Meantime Phil May joined the staff of the *Graphic*, occasionally also working for *Pick-Me-Up*. His first drawings for the *Graphic* appeared in the November 1890 issue under the title "A Day with a Medicine Man". They depicted an American quack, Sequah, touting potions across the States, relying heavily on crooked publicity and false gimmickry. Perhaps Phil May had someone like Horatio Bottomley on his mind: in every town the arch-villain Sequah visited, processions were organised and bands boomed to mark his arrival — yet all he did was cheat money from his victims.

An interesting thing about the Sequah drawings was that they were reproduced in their original size rather than being reduced in the engraving, as was usual. Another commission from the *Graphic* was to sketch a children's annual fancy-dress ball at the Mansion House, a pleasant task for Phil, who loved children. One young mother who noticed him sketching her son asked to see the result. Phil showed her the sketch and was surprised when she pressed a half-crown into his hand: she was so pleased with his effort and the fact that he was immortalising her child in the pages of the *Graphic* that she had felt obliged to tip him. Not wishing to cause offence, Phil graciously accepted the offering. Later he retold the story with glee in the confines of the Savage Club bar, producing the coin from his waistcoat pocket to emphasise the point.

His finances were to improve greatly during 1891, the year in which *The Parson and the Painter* appeared in book form. The first impression of ten thousand copies sold in a flash, fifteen hundred from one York bookstall alone, and the publisher proposed reprinting on a royalty basis. Eventually thirty thousand copies were sold in spite of the opposition of an eminent church dignitary who succeeded in banning the publication from railway bookstalls. Originally published at one shilling, copies are now worth something like £30. Perhaps the work will be republished one day, if only as a sparkling record of Victorian life.

The *Daily Chronicle* acclaimed the book in a three-column review, describing Phil May as "a new artist" — much to Allison's disgust, who had been publishing his drawings for eight years. This review did May's reputation an immense amount of good, firmly establishing his career. The profits from *The Parson and the Painter*, together with his regular income, made life much easier for Phil, who had never had so much money in his life. With the unexpected windfall he could now afford to buy Lilian a house — and he could also buy himself a horse. From his boyhood days, he had always wanted a horse. He had ridden a pony with his paternal grandfather's pack of beagles in Derbyshire on very special holidays when his parents had gone to stay with Charles Hughes May, the squire of Whittington. Unhappily Phil's father had dissipated any inheritance Phil might have received from his wealthy, landowning grandfather.

SOUVENIR OF HYÈRES

THE OCTROI—*Sketch in Paris*

Early in 1892 the Mays moved to their new house at 7 Holland Park Road. It had a large studio, and offered comfort and space undreamed of when they had moved into the cramped flat in Covent Garden. It was also more amenable to the bohemian graphic set who mostly lived in Holland Park, Chelsea and Kensington. Besides which, it had ample stabling at the back for the new horse.

On January 28th 1893 Phil May was nominated for the Savage Club, his election being confirmed two months later when Edgar "Tasker" Lee proposed him and he was seconded by A. C. Corbould and Thomas Henry. Thomas Henry was a mediocre painter and illustrator who flourished at the turn of the century, while A. C. Corbould was to become a firm friend of May's for the rest of Phil's life. The two were great drinking companions. May had always admired Corbould's famous uncle, Charles Keene, through whose introduction Corbould knew most of the *Punch* men. Corbould was a great club man, the Savage being one of his favourite haunts, and he and Phil would talk into the small hours within its safe confines.

Soon after buying his horse, Phil May was riding to the offices of the *Graphic* when he decided to drop in at the Savage Club. He left his horse with a man outside, instructing him to walk the animal up and down until his return. It was lunchtime and on entering the club he was soon surrounded by a crowd of friends and acquaintances, which prompted the need for refreshment. Phil became so pre-occupied with the bonhomie of his fellow clubmen that he forgot all about his horse, and when it was time to leave he proceeded to the office on foot. The man holding his horse became anxious for his tip and asked the hall porter if Mr May was still in the club. "No," replied the porter, "he left an hour ago!" Other members were consulted and eventually Phil's horse was put in a livery stable around the corner.

Several days elapsed before Phil again appeared at the club. "Most extra-ordinary thing," he said, "I've lost my horse!"

With his new affluence, Phil's drinking bouts became more frequent and more prolonged. One morning, when he should have been working on a drawing for *Graphic*, he went out for a walk instead. It took him along the Strand. Calling at regular haunts, he drank his way through the afternoon and well into the night. When he returned home in the small hours he tip-toed through the studio and crept into bed silently without waking Lilian. Or so he thought. Next morning when Lilian was up and about, he opened one eye, and was just about to get out of bed when he heard her say, "Rest for a bit this morning, dear, you were very late last night."

"But my *Graphic* drawing... I've got to get it done..." responded Phil, half asleep.

"My dear, you finished the drawing last night before coming to bed. It's on the easel in the studio."

Lilian was well aware of her husband's gregariousness and generosity. Once he got into a bar there was no stopping him, and Phil May's London was strewn with bars of every description. The Strand was a particularly dangerous spot, but since his office lay in its vicinity, it could not be avoided. From the Silver Grill to the Cheshire Cheese, it was one long gin crawl. Then there was Romano's, where "Auntie" presided over many a famous man from the worlds of sport, drama, literature and art, and there was the old Gaiety Bar, and the Tivoli across the road. Tucked away were the Caledonian and the Adelphi, and after the theatre there was the Coal Hole, where a coterie of the acting fraternity formed a friendly symposium. Last but not least was the Savage Club itself, offering an ever-open door to the weary and thirsty traveller. This was Phil May's real world. Wherever he went

he was recognised, and he enjoyed the affection people lavished on him. In every lounge he reigned supreme. He had his own group of admirers whom J. B. Booth described as "parasites and hangers-on". Keble Howard called them "his little group of friends", while James Thorpe politely named them "his large circle of acquaintances". He was a prime target for any scrounger, or for anyone who possessed a power of rhetoric to match his own wit.

In 1893 W. L. Thomas, founder of the *Graphic* and *Daily Graphic* decided to send Phil May to the World's Fair in Chicago. E. S. Grew of the literary staff was chosen to accompany him and it was hoped that between them they would provide enough material for several months. A draft of a letter written in one of Phil May's sketch books gives a dismal account of the voyage:

Arrived on board and found letter from Thomas wishing us God-speed. Also two boxes of cigars, one for Grew and one for myself, from Harvey Thomas. We started from Southampton at 12 o'clock. Sorry to find did not stop at Queenstown; beautiful weather until we got past Cornwall. Since then most awful passage I have had. We have both been very sick. The morning after we left it was blowing a gale. I tried to have some breakfast and managed a little but everything was so sickly that I couldn't manage much. Fancy steak and eggs for a sick man! Lunch no better. How would you like some roast lamb and stewed prunes mixed? It turned me up again. Dinner I was feeling very qualmsy but they brought me some roast goose and stewed apricots and cherries. The Germans seem to eat fruit instead of vegetables with viands. Whatever you do don't

Minister: "Hoo is't, Sandy, I never see you at the Kirk, the noo?"

Sandy: "I canna stand your long sermons."

Minister: "Ah, weel! Ye'll be goin' to a place where there'll be no sermons at all, neither lang nor short."

Sandy: "It'll nay be for the want o' Meenisters, then!"

Father O'Flynn: "Pat, you're dhrunk again."

Pat: "Oi'm not, yer Riverence."

Father O'Flynn: "Yis ye are, Pat; an' if ye were not, you wouldn't deny it."

WE MUSTN'T ALWAYS JUDGE BY APPEARANCES

"I say, Bill, you aren't got such a thing as the price of 'arf a pint about you, are yer? I'm so bloomin' *dry*!"

come by German boat. The company on this ship is awful. I never met such a lot of German and American cads in my life. We have both been too ill to work, but are now getting used to the motion — but it's terrible.

The German liner *Columbia* carried an assortment of Continental characters from German Jews to red-nosed Tyroleans in hunting caps. Even a Russian journalist mixed with these ambitious hopefuls as they ploughed their way across the Atlantic to discover a new land. A military band added pomp and ceremony, playing — much to Phil's disgust — most of the time. Neither Phil May nor Grew enjoyed the journey and they would both frequently retire to the bar to partake of refreshment to console their rough passage. After docking in New York they were conned by a professional joke purveyor. It was the last straw.

In New York Phil sauntered into a police court where a coloured woman was up before the magistrate on a charge of being drunk and disorderly, a charge which she denied.

"How do you know she was drunk?" asked the magistrate.

"She walked into a bakery," replied the policeman giving evidence, "to buy a bonnet!"

The evidence was accepted as being conclusive. Phil dashed off a quick sketch of the woman which he used in "The Gutterwoman", his first contribution to *Punch;* it was also republished as a sketch in the *Graphic.*

Although May worked well on board ship and in New York, Chicago was a different matter. The World's Fair was never covered by the *Graphic* because the pickling process which had begun at sea got out of hand during the rest of his and Grew's stay in America. From New York to Chicago a monumental binge was ferociously sustained, Grew being easily led by May down the slippery slope. Phil insisted that America did not agree with him, but it was a feeble excuse. The two men returned home via a westerly route, so making theirs a round-the-world cruise.

The two sobered travellers returned on July 6th 1893 and mounted the stairs of the *Graphic* to face the music. Like two truant schoolboys they cautiously entered the proprietor's office to confront a furious Thomas. It so happened that July 6th was also the wedding day of Prince George and Princess May, so the initials "G" and "M" blazed and fluttered everywhere. Before Thomas had a chance to open his mouth, Phil May exclaimed: "This is most handsome of you — absolutely wonderful — we never expected such a reception. All these flags and things — must have cost you a fortune — and our initials too all along the street." The astounded editor was shaken heartily by the hand and was so taken aback that after a few seconds he burst into laughter at the return of his prodigals.

The card for the Phil May Exhibition at the Leicester Galleries

5   Holland Park

Y 1892 Phil May was contributing work to most of the London illustrated papers, including *The Illustrated London News*. His fame was increasing, as were callers to the welcoming door of 7 Holland Park Road. The studio was a well-known haunt for Sunday afternoon parties. Phil greatly enjoyed these informal "at homes" when singers, actors, writers and painters would pop in for a casual drink. The great impromptu actor Dudley Hardy was a frequent visitor, and so too was the portrait painter Edwin Ward.

One evening a well-known Spanish dancer, accompanied by her husband and her business manager, arrived at the house, clutching a handbag full of valuable jewellery. The harmony of the gathering was suddenly interrupted by the outbreak of a violent quarrel between her two escorts. They had to be separated by other guests: the husband was kept in the dining-room downstairs while the manager was asked to leave. He was eventually persuaded to go, after issuing many verbal threats, and soon afterwards the dancer and her husband departed in a hansom. Almost immediately, however, they were back, announcing that her jewellery was missing. Consternation appeared on the guests' faces as they glanced suspiciously at each other. What was to be done? Lilian was distraught and even Phil's usually imperturbable smile had disappeared as a feeling of unease spread over the assembly. The house was searched, to no avail, when some bright spark suggested they look in the hansom cab which was waiting outside. The bag of jewellery was found on the floor of the cab, its contents intact. Profuse Iberian apologies were accepted with enormous relief.

Soirées of this sort at 7 Holland Park Road eventually deteriorated into bouts of alcoholic excess. At one end of the studio a barrel of whisky surrounded by syphons and tumblers would be provided for guests. At first this seemed an excellent arrangement, but after a while word seemed to get round to every bar and club parasite in London, who could smell free whisky miles away. They descended in hordes and the barrel was soon empty. Sunday afternoons degenerated to such an extent that the whisky barrel had to be renewed more than once during the course of the party. To make matters worse, the spongers began to cadge or steal drawings, and almost anything else they could lay their hands on. Phil's real friends began leaving their wives at home, and soon began to stay away themselves. Edwin Ward recalled one of these parties in *Recollections of a Savage*:

> I call to mind one evening at his house in the Holland Park Road; the dining-room was crowded with noisy revellers helping themselves freely to a hospitality which was always boundless, when Phil, taking me away by the arm, led me upstairs into his working-room. What a contrast to the rowdy scene down below! Every detail necessary for the practice of his masterly draughtsmanship was in perfect order, and with simple pride he described to me his method of work. Nothing appeared to be left to chance. He proceeded to illustrate the process by which he had arrived at his ultimate simplicity of line. Over an elaborate drawing he stretched a sheet of tracing paper, and found that by eliminating all superfluous detail he could present his picture with greater force and directness.

A GREAT DISAPPOINTMENT

Proud Parent (who has been introducing his son to some of England's gentlemen): "THERE, MY BOY, THIS WILL BE SOMETHING FOR YOU TO REMEMBER WHEN YOU ARE A MAN!"

Young Hopeful (rather disappointed): "ISN'T THERE A *CONJURER* AMONGST THEM?"

An August Bank-holiday in the East End
(From "The Century Magazine")

A Street Row in the East End
(From "The Century Magazine")

The sloping desk at which he worked was for all the world like a lectern, and Phil himself, sitting there quietly explaining the process by which these wonderful drawings were evolved was, with head bowed over his papers and books, curiously reminiscent of His Holiness Pope Pius the Ninth. Oddly enough he had at times himself slyly traced a humorous resemblance in their profiles. Crooning away in the musical voice it was a pleasure to listen to, there he sat turning over the leaves of a folio of sketches with his exquisitely formed hands, hands that any woman might be proud to possess.

He was happy as a child in escaping for a moment from the smoke and din downstairs, the noise of which just reached us through the closed door. Then, as though a little ashamed of having been discovered — like a shy girl caught reading a love letter — he closed the folio and, getting down from his desk, said: "What a shame, you must be feeling thirsty." Turning down the light in his sanctum, he led me back again to the blarers in the room below. It was the only occasion upon which I saw, and then only for a moment, a glimpse of the real Phil May — the greatest artist in black and white of all time.

Before the decline of these parties, when spoof-players provided the entertainment, Phil loved to take part in the games himself. He would do conjuring tricks and, on one occasion, gave an exhibition of thought-reading. He persuaded a lady to take a card and think hard about it. He left the room — only to be press-ganged by Dudley Hardy, who was concocting a stirring drama. After ten minutes he returned to find the lady, still concentrating on her card, in imminent danger of collapse. She accepted his profuse apologies and the party continued.

On some occasions Phil would entertain his guests by whistling or singing. He loved the songs of Sims Reeves which he delivered in a pleasant tenor voice. Few people connect Phil May's name with music, but he composed two songs which were published by Boosey & Company, "The Roses That I Gave To You" and "Souvenir". A rough draft of the words of the first of these was found in one of his sketch books:

> The roses that I gave to you
> E'en yesterday, all fresh with dew,
> Lie withered now and scentless too.
> Hear me, Lilian, speaking sooth,
> Gather the flowers of your youth
> Ere they wither as they must:
> Nothing lingers here but dust.
> So do not waste a single minute,
> But gather all the joy that's in it.

Two other friends who enjoyed these early gatherings were Charles Bertram and Walter Churcher, both fellow-members of the Savage Club. Walter Churcher was an excellent raconteur, while Charles Bertram was a famous conjurer. Phil May tried to imitate Bertram's sleight of hand, but only succeeded in achieving some very ham-fisted results. Bertram had a remarkable career, from his early days as a partner in the ownership of a chain of public houses to the lawsuit that followed, and subsequent ruin. He drifted into conjuring as a way of passing the time. As a result of the intervention of Edward VII, then Prince of Wales, Bertram entertained at a royal banquet. This success assured him endless work, including many a Royal Command. According to Edwin Ward, he was "without a rival in his own time". Unfortunately, he invested his new-found wealth in a collapsible car invented by fellow Savage Club member van der Weyed, but the project, like the car, eventually collapsed. Bertram lost everything, and died soon afterwards in poverty.

Walter Churcher, who lived in Bedford Park, was an ardent contributor to the London press, and would recite enthusiastically at Phil's informal gatherings. While the Mays collected blue-and-white Chinese porcelain, Churcher collected pewter. His collection of pewter snuff boxes fascinated Lilian and when he visited the Holland Park studio he would bring different varieties to show her.

Lilian had enjoyed the Sunday get-togethers in the early days and had circulated among her guests happily chatting to the varied characters. As the parties grew more unruly, however, she anxiously watched the studio and gallery in an effort to prevent guests helping themselves to Phil's drawings. One method of saving at least some of them was to persuade Phil to write on the backs: "To Lil". Then, if she saw one of these drawings being appropriated she could point to the inscription and claim it back. If Phil gave anything to Lilian, he was adamant about her rights to it.

Nevertheless, many Phil May drawings found their way to the pawnshop in the Strand situated conveniently opposite Romano's. Here so-called friends could exchange their plunder for cash, though most of these drawings realised very much less than their true value. Some "friends" even went to the lengths of forging Phil's signature on bills, confident in the knowledge that he wouldn't remember whether he had signed them or not. As one friend of the time wrote, "Some respected his simplicity, fostering his genius, and striving their utmost to keep the curs, that hungry pack, at bay." But the curs continued to flourish and a considerable number of forged Phil May drawings were produced. These can easily be detected by the hesitancy and weakness of line compared with the confidence and proficiency of Phil May's real work. Phil was not offended by this dishonesty but accepted imitation as the sincerest form of flattery. And he forever under-estimated his own worth. A friend once asked him why he did so little "serious" work. "Ah!" he replied, with whimsical self-deprication, "if you're going to be serious, you've got to be so dam' good."

Phil May's philosophy of art was best summed up by Frank Brangwyn:

> We must never forget that the great artists of the past were, first and foremost, honest, capable craftsmen, who worked to the order of various patrons and clients. Isn't it nonsense to talk, as the "highbrows" do, of "prostituting your art" when you work for a businessman? Obviously you only prostitute Art when you do it badly. As to selling your work, it is quite immaterial whether your client is a king, a bishop or a soap-boiler, as long as your work is really worthy of you. There should be a lot more commonsense in Art, and less affectation; and perhaps the worst affectation is this nonsense about "vulgarising" Art by associating it with commerce. I want to see it used a great deal more, not only for Commerce but for *Life*. I want it to be more useful and comforting to the people. What is Art, if it is not a message that everybody can understand? Did Rubens, or Titian, or Rembrandt mystify the public or sneer at them? They did not. Did they set themselves on pedestals — or pose — or paint down to the public level? They did not. The public is quite ready for the finest Art that any living artist can offer. And we shall certainly get more commonsense into Advertising when the Artist and the Businessman are better friends.

 One of Phil May's most commercially successful protégés was the bohemian reprobate James Pryde. The Pride-Nicholson partnership was paraded under the name of "The Beggarstaff Brothers". They produced a Cinderella poster for Sir Augustus Harris in Drury Lane which was at first ridiculed by all who saw it. However, it reminded May of his early efforts for the Grand Theatre in Leeds when he was prompted to do a similar poster for *Bo-Peep*. While at the theatre where he had first seen the Cinderella poster, he noticed Augustus Harris and went up to him

"GENTLEMEN, I AM READY TO ADMIT THAT HIS CAREER IN THE PAST HAS NOT BEEN FREE FROM BLEMISH—"

OVERHEARD ON A RECENT MUDDY DAY

Old Lady: "I DON'T SEE THE CROSSING-SWEEPER HERE TODAY, POLICEMAN!"

Policeman: "NO, MUM. HE'S OUT MARCHING WITH THE UNEMPLOYED TODAY."

LA VIE DE BOHEME

First Bohemian (to second ditto): "I CAN'T FOR THE LIFE OF ME THINK WHY YOU WASTED ALL THAT TIME HAGGLING WITH THAT TAILOR CHAP, AND BEATING HIM DOWN, WHEN YOU KNOW, OLD CHAP, YOU WON'T BE ABLE TO PAY HIM AT ALL."

Second Bohemian: "AH, THAT'S IT! I HAVE A CONSCIENCE. I WANT THE POOR CHAP TO LOSE AS LITTLE AS POSSIBLE!"

Lady Customer (at Bric-a-brac Shop): "I THINK YOU ARE VERY, VERY DEAR!"

Proprietor: "HUSH! NOT SO LOUD, MISS. MY OLD 'OMAN BE POWERFUL JEALOUS!"

The Fortune Teller

"Here's a Health unto His Majesty"

Harmony

From "The Phil May Folio."

Phrenologist (to Park Loafer): "Now, you're full o' nerves, you are. What you want is Iron; you mus'n't drink Beer; you must drink Burgundy."

immediately, shaking him confidently by the hand, and congratulated him on a brilliant poster. Much to the delight of the Beggarstaff Brothers it was then placed on the hoardings outside the theatre. Later, in an interview with the *Idler*, the Beggarstaff Brothers expressed their gratitude to May, saying, "There is one thing you must not forget to mention and that is the great help we have received from Phil May, one of the kindest and best friends we have had throughout."

While working on the *Graphic*, Phil May struck up a warm friendship with Harvey Thomas, son of the founder, as well as with its stable of artists which included A. S. Hartrick, E. J. Sullivan and Frank Dean. Hartrick was so influenced by May that his pen drawings almost lost the stamp of his own style, though he held his own in the medium of chalk. Phil May was delighted with this new medium and quickly adopted it for his genre scenes of brazen Cockney showgirls and coster-mongers. Dean, who shared a flat with Sullivan, was, like Phil himself, from Leeds. They were about the same age and had been in Paris together, though Dean's training there differed somewhat from May's haphazard studentship. He had studied under the celebrated Boulanger, as indeed had Hartrick. Sullivan achieved some success as a book illustrator. Although eclipsed by contemporaries such as Rackham and Dulac, he was a fine artist and a talented lecturer, remembered for his fluent teaching of book illustration and lithography at Goldsmiths' College of Art until his death in 1933. He no doubt left a lasting imprint on twentieth-century graphics.

Later artists who worked for the *Graphic* included Robert Baden-Powell, John Hassall, Reginald Cleaver and A. C. Corbould. Phil May's advice to less exper-ienced artists was to "draw from life and keep drawing from life". Observation was the keynote of his own art and he would himself fill literally hundreds of sketch pads and notebooks with doodles and delicate drawings which could be drawn upon for his cartoons at some later date. Among Victorian black-and-white artists only Charles Keene came near to rivalling Phil May in accomplishment. As one contemporary critic noted, "No draughtsman has ever equalled Phil May's vigorous and assured control of a pen. It is remarkable that this wonderful strength should have emanated from so physically frail a source." Keene used to modify the colour of his ink lines to suggest tone, whereas May relied on line alone and achieved an equally brilliant finish. Personally, I prefer the clean-cut, crisp character of May's penmanship to the fuzziness of Keene's tonal drawing. If Keene was the better "artist", May was nevertheless the better draughtsman, and certainly the greater humourist. When members of the Savage Club were debating which of the two was better, Phil himself settled the matter in a characteristic way: "I am, of course!" he pronounced. "Keene's dead!"

One of May's early commissions for the *Graphic* was to cover a Mayoral procession. He ensconced himself in one of the window recesses at Romano's, from which he had a good view of the street and, "for the good of the house", as the phrase goes, ordered a bottle of champagne which stood beside him as he sketched. Engrossed in his work, he was suddenly aware of a hand thrusting over his shoulder and seizing his bottle. Turning his head, he observed a stranger helping himself to a glass of his champagne. Odd things frequently happened to Phil, and he didn't begrudge anybody a drink, so, since the bottle was duly returned to its place, he took no notice and carried on working. Soon the same hand took the bottle once more so that even the easy going Phil was impelled to remark, "You seem to like that champagne!"

"Yes," agreed the stranger briskly, "first-rate stuff."

"It ought to be," retorted Phil. "Cost me fifteen shillings!" (This was the most expensive champagne, even at Romano's, during the 'nineties.)

The stranger's jaw dropped. With a blank expression on his face he spluttered, "I... I beg your pardon, Mr May... really I do beg your pardon. I thought this was Romano's treat!" Romano on occasions *would* dispense a bottle at his own expense if trade seemed slow, or on festive days. "I do beg your pardon," repeated the abashed stranger. "I hope you'll accept my apologies, Mr May. I can't say how sorry I am. I... I... Look here... will you do me a favour, Mr May... a great favour? Will you allow me to offer you a cigar?"

The kindly Phil was so overwhelmed by these apologies he almost felt like apologising himself. "Oh, it's all right..." he replied. "Don't bother."

But the man insisted. "Here, Miss Hunty," he called to the barmaid. "Three cigars please... the best... the best in the place, of course." From some deep recess behind the bar came a soberly expensive looking box of very large Havanas. Phil took one, the stranger and his friend one each. Lights were applied. The stranger clapped his hand to his pocket: "How much?" he asked.

"Twenty-two and sixpence, Sir."

For a second his jaw dropped again. His little error had been expensive, but he paid up like a Briton.

May, whose sketches had gone as far as was necessary, strolled out into the Strand with his portfolio under his arm and the dearest cigar of his experience in his mouth. He walked to the Strand Theatre, where he poked his head round the door of the manager's office. The manager, Mr Bicknell Smith, was an impetuous body; he deftly snatched the cigar out of Phil May's mouth and flung it on the fire. "Here, Phil," he shouted hospitably, "have a *good* one!" and presented his own box of very ordinary office smokes.

A hundred yards further along the Strand, May met A. C. Corbould. "Did you ever smoke a seven-and-sixpenny cigar?" was his greeting.

"Never."

"I have... for nearly five minutes; and if you'd like to smell it you must hurry... it's on Bicknell Smith's fire!"

The legend of Phil May's lifestyle had by this time become established. No doubt many of the stories about him which circulated were quite true, and even those told in jest had some element of truth in them. One such story concerned the Holland Arms, where Phil would go for an early morning drink. Before 1914, when licensing hours were introduced, there was little or no restriction. Phil had long frequented the pubs in the Strand area, but his move to Holland Park had widened his network of "quick stops". Cecil Aldin, who lived in a small house with a large studio and yard in Bedford Park, also frequented the Holland Arms. "Morning, Phil," he said one morning as he walked in.

"And what's yours?" was Phil's customary reply.

After a while Aldin noticed Phil saying "And what's yours?" to everyone who came into the bar, and asked him if he really knew all those people.

"I can't remember having seen any of them before," Phil confessed. But he kept on buying them drinks.

When he left the Holland Arms he bumped into a policeman. Just what he wanted! He asked the constable if he would be kind enough to pose for him when he came off duty. Naturally Phil took advantage of one or two more "quick stops" before getting home, and he encountered several more policemen, each of whom was asked the same question.

"IF I WOS YOU I WOULDN'T 'AVE NOTHING TO DO WITH
MRS SMITH; I THINK SHE AIN'T RESPECTABLE."

Youngster: "FATHER, TEACHER SAYS I'VE GOTTEN TER
BRING A PENNY WI' ME TO SCHOOL TERMORRER TER BUY
A SLATE PENCIL WI'!"
Parent: "GO IT! GO IT!! THAT MAK'S NINEPENCE-A'PENNY
I'VE SPENT ON YER EDICATION ALREADY."

OVERHEARD ON A CAB RANK

"'AVE YER SEEN ANYTHING OF WHATYERCALLIM?"
"WHO? D'YE MEAN WHATSISNAME?"
"OH, NO, NOT 'IM — THAT 'ERE T'OTHER."
"OH, AH — I SEED 'IM FAST ENOUGH!"

Bill Snooks (reading from a fashion paper): "'TO BE
REALLY WELL DRESSED A MAN'S CLOTHES SHOULD
HAVE THE APPEARANCE OF HAVING BEEN WORN ONCE
OR TWICE.' WHAT *O!*"

From "The Phil May Folio"

By the time he returned to his studio there was quite a posse of policemen gathered outside. "Good God!" exclaimed Phil, "what's wrong — is there a fire?"

Another morning, when Phil was suffering a worse hangover than usual, he decided to stop in bed. Lilian, who was up and about early, busying herself in the kitchen, decided the cupboard needed replenishing. She went into the bedroom to ask Phil for some money. He lay in an abysmal state, cradling his aching head. Gathering his tattered thoughts, he realised he had spent all his money on the previous night's booze. "I'm sorry, I haven't any," came the muffled reply from beneath the bedclothes.

But Lilian thought to herself. "Never mind, dear," she answered. "Remember that double-page spread you did for the Christmas number of the *Graphic*? They still owe you for that, so you stop in bed and I'll pop along to the office and draw the money."

This was rather awkward for Phil, who had not only had the money already, but spent it. The moment his wife had left the house, he jumped out of bed, put on a hat and overcoat, seized his stick, hailed a passing hansom and got to the *Graphic* office before Lilian, who was still waiting for the omnibus. "Look here, old man," he said to the editor, "I wonder if you could do me a favour. You know that double-page I did for the Christmas number?"

"Yes, Phil, the one I've just paid you for."

"Yes, that one. I know you've paid me for it — but my wife doesn't know it, and she's coming along to collect the money at this very minute. For God's sake pay her, and I'll do you another drawing."

The editor agreed, and Phil went back to bed.

Shortly afterwards Lilian arrived at the *Graphic* office and was shown up to the editorial sanctum. She stated her business and was paid, but just as she was about to leave she noticed a walking-stick in the hat stand. "Good heavens!" she cried, "how in the world did that get here?"

"That?" parried the editor. "Oh, I suppose some visitor must have left it."

"That stick belongs to Phil," she pronounced. "There's not another like it in London. And less than an hour ago I saw it standing by his bedside!"

It was not the first time that Phil had been rumbled. Although he was quick-witted he invariably tripped himself up like a music-hall clown so that his ploys were doomed from the start. Lilian must have been a wife in a million to put up with her husband's impossibly irregular hours and wanton generosity to strangers.

Phil May's haunts in the artist's London must have matched up pretty well to anything that Paris could offer. Romano's surely boasted just as many characters as the Moulin Rouge, while Holland Park could equal Montmartre as a stamping ground for artists. There was a peculiarly English eccentricity to be found in the bohemian bars and clubs of London which rivalled Parisian counterparts in colourfulness. Though London may have lacked the promiscuous sparkle exuding out of "Gay Paree", it had its own music-hall jollity and naughtiness, as well as the ambiguous humour of Gilbert and Sullivan and the highbrow wit of Oscar Wilde.

One of Phil May's favourite restaurants in London was Pagani's in Great Portland Street. Opened in 1871 by Mario Pagani, an Italian caterer, it grew from a small *patisserie* into a thriving and classy restaurant. The clientèle were mainly painters, writers and singers, and regulars included Tosti, George Sims and the great *Vanity Fair* caricaturist Carlo Pellegrini. Better known as "Ape", Pellegrini was instrumental in reviving the British interest in caricature. He was a great influence not only on his understudy Sir Leslie Ward ("Spy" of the *Graphic*), but

*From a panel at Pagani's,
Great Portland Street, W.*

also Max Beerbohm, who dedicated his first book to him in 1896. Unhappily Pellegrini had died in 1889 in difficult financial circumstances. Pagani himself had passed away already in 1887, the restaurant being carried on by his brother and a cousin. Over the next few years Pagani's underwent many changes, increasing in size and degree of ornamentation, but it retained its Italian flavour. Its waiters, who generally sported Continental moustaches, were of obviously Italian origin, while all specialities on the menu were indigenous to that country.

One night when Phil had just dined at Pagani's in his usual inebriated state, he tipped one of the waiters with a ten-pound note. "What's the largest tip you've ever received?" he asked.

"Thees ees, Sir," replied the waiter.

"And what was it before?"

"Onlys fiv'a pound'as," replied the waiter obediently, and Phil's chest expanded with pride.

"Who gave you that?"

"You did'a, Sir."

"Don't 'e make a gawd of 'is stummick? Why, that's the *second* 'a'porth I've seed 'im 'ave this mornin'!"

From "The Phil May Folio"

"Do you want a errand boy?"
"No."
"Yus you do, yours 'as just been runned over."

A LARGE ORDER

Little Girl: "Three penn'orth o' brandy; an' I want a cork; an' will ye wash the bottle out, 'cos it's 'ad milk in it."

This little scene took place in a room on the second floor of Pagani's, known as the Artists' Room. Its walls were covered with autographs, sketches, photographs and pages of musical manuscripts. Caruso would often dine here after singing at Covent Garden; Mascagni had written out the first bars of "Cavalleria Rusticana" here, and indeed they were now pinned to one of the walls, as was a caricature of the great Caruso, donated by himself. Among the nostalgic conglomeration of other offerings were the autographs of Tschaikovsky, Puccini, Paderewski, Chaminade and Melba, and, among the many photographs, a large autographed portrait of Henry Irving as Becket, and one of Phil May on his horse Punch. Sadly, this delightful corner of artistic bohemia was bombed during the blitz.

It was through May's association with Pagani's that he was drawn into a swinging musical set. He produced a popular series called "Singers and Their Songs" for *Punch*, having found the inspiration for one of these sketches during a dinner at the Savoy. As T. C. Bridges explained in *From Florida to Fleet Street*:

> Phil May was asked to a supper party at the Savoy, given in honour of a great singer, and afterwards did a dainty little drawing on the menu of the guest of the evening. This was passed round for inspection and presently fell into the hands of a woman whose wealth was only equalled by her lack of breeding. She called a waiter, handed the man a ten-pound note and told him to "Take it to Mr May and ask him to do me a similar drawing". Note and message were duly delivered and the sender was gratified by seeing the artist rise to his feet and take a good look at her. Then he set to work, and in a little while the waiter returned to the sender with the result. It was a caricature — an appallingly truthful caricature — and it was executed on the back of the ten-pound note.

There are many amusing incidents connected with Phil May's work. George Robey, that great old music-hall comedian, often told a story about May's "Dottyville" series which appeared in *Punch*. Someone from Hanwell Asylum was so incensed by one of the cartoons that he wrote to May:

> I greatly resent those sketches. You apparently do not understand your subject, for you have drawn the head of an idiot and labelled it a lunatic. You ought to know the difference — but you don't. And I'm not surprised because, having seen your photograph, I have noted your's is the head of an idiot.

Reading this letter, Phil asked a friend, "Who is this lunatic?"

"Oh, the man who wrote that letter was no lunatic," replied the friend. "He was the Warden!"

George Robey once painted a sign reading "DOTTYVILLE" in large red letters and, helped by accomplices, attached it to Phil's front gate in the early hours of one morning. Phil transferred it to the door of his studio, where it remained some time. The "Dottyville" series was a great favourite in *Punch*; some of the sketches (such as the actor who often heard of salaries of twenty-five or thirty bob a week but never saw them, or the bibulous gentleman at the railway station bar who was asked whether he wanted tea and replied, "Tea! Me!!!!") are perfect. My personal favourites are "A Friend in Need", "Q.E.D." and "Foggy Weather", but perhaps the most lovable cartoon is the one of the bedraggled woman being ejected from a Gin Palace, saying, "*Next* time I goes into a Publick House — I'll go somewhere where I'll be respected!"

6 The Election to "Punch"

VERY SOON AFTER Phil May joined the staff of *Punch* in 1895, M. H. Spielmann, who wrote *The History of "Punch"*, recorded: "*Punch* was long in discovering him, but he found him at last. Indeed, he could not afford to do without him, for Mr May, though barely more than thirty years of age, was already in the foremost rank of the humorous draughtsmen of the day." May's first contribution to the celebrated weekly had appeared in the issue of October 14th 1893.

As part of the required ritual, he carefully carved his initials on the famous table in February 1895, when he first sat down to dine among this distinguished set of literary jokers and staid illustrators. He was slightly nervous, rather shy and very overawed by the traditions of such a famous group. He sat at the deal table, roughly shaped like a running track, with Lawrence Bradbury on one side of him and Bernard Partridge on the other, and listened to the week's business. When it was time to discuss the subject of the following week's political cartoon, the editor, F. C. Burnand, rose to his feet with customary aplomb. "Gentlemen, the cartoon!" he announced, as the company pushed aside the ruined remnants of cheese and lit up their cigars. The first few minutes after a generous meal are not the best time to discuss weighty matters, and at future meetings May was reputed generally to have slid under the table at this juncture; however, on this first occasion, he was unusually sober. It was only when everyone was leaving that he turned quietly to Bernard Partridge and ventured: "Let's go to Romano's for a drink!"

May was proud to have joined so noble a gathering. The election to *Punch* was the highest accolade of black-and-white artists, though when he joined he was still very much the outsider. When his friend M. H. Spielmann wrote to congratulate him on his success, Phil May replied: "I joined the *Punch* staff last week and dined with them last Wednesday, and carved my name on the scroll of fame! I mean the dining table. It has made me awfully happy."

Phil May's tradition of drunkenness while with *Punch* is still remembered: it was even suggested that at the first dinner he was so incapacitated as to have signed his initials *under* the famous table. A better substantiated story concerned the illustrations for one December number of *Punch*. As time grew short, the editor was alarmed to discover that Phil had vanished to Margate and gone to ground. In desperation he employed a sandwich-board man to parade the streets of Margate with the message, "Remember the Christmas issue!"

Phil's bouts of "going to ground" were attempts to keep as far away from any bar as possible. His drinks-all-round philosophy made him so popular, however, that it was an almost impossible task to escape the chain of friends and endless quick stops. To get away from it all and try to get some work done, he took the extreme step of renting a studio in Paris. Both he and Lilian had fond memories of their stay there in 1889, when they had watched the completion of the Eiffel Tower, and there was the added advantage that Phil was little known in Paris.

AT A LITERARY AND ARTISTIC BANQUET

Waiter (to Colleague): "WELL, THEY MAY 'AVE THE INTELLEC', FRED, BUT WE CERTAINLY
'AS THE GOOD LOOKS!"

Little Griggs (to caricaturist): "BY JOVE, OLD FELLER I
WISH YOU'D BEEN WITH ME THIS MORNING; YOU'D HAVE
SEEN SUCH A FUNNY LOOKING CHAP!"

Patient: "WHAT WOULD YOU THINK OF A WARMER
CLIMATE FOR ME, DOCTOR?"
Doctor: "GOOD HEAVENS, SIR, THAT'S JUST WHAT I AM
TRYING TO SAVE YOU FROM!"

On one occasion, however, when he was making his way to his new studio, Phil May broke his journey at Etaples to call on Dudley Hardy. "Why are you going to Paris?" asked Hardy.

"I've been so overwhelmed by a flock of 'good fellows'," explained Phil, "that work is really out of the question, and my only chance of freedom is to remove myself from their reach."

Dudley Hardy had just received a cheque for £50 and, as he had no bank account in Etaples and wanted to cash it urgently, was faced with a problem. "It's all right, Dudley," replied Phil, "I'll cash it for you in Paris and bring you the money on my way back."

"Well, if you're going down to Paris, I'll come with you," decided Dudley, and the two friends set off for the capital.

Once in Paris, they not only cashed the cheque but spent the money. As Phil later remarked, "We had a wild day!" The resulting hangover left him in no fit state to accomplish his weekly *Punch* cartoon. Dudley Hardy, who was clearly made of stronger stuff, offered to do it for him — indeed, that particular cartoon, though it bears Phil May's signature, is by Hardy.

In spite of such irregularities, Phil May's work for *Punch* was enormously appreciated, and was in fact regularly produced. "One marvels at the vast amount of work he did," remarked Sir Henry Lucy ("Toby, M.P.") "Messengers were often sent with orders to stay on the doorstep until the drawing was finished." This is reminiscent of the grand tradition of John Leech, who frequently kept the first editor of *Punch*, Mark Lemon, waiting for his work. As Edmund Yates recorded: "Half of Mark Lemon's time was spent in hansom cabs

The "Punch" Table
1895 or early 1896

From left clockwise: E. J. Milliken, George Du Maurier, Arthur A. Beckett, Linley Sambourne, Sir John Tenniel, F. C. Burnand, F. Anstey, Henry Lucy, Phil May

Genial Doctor (after laughing at a joke of his patient's): "HA! HA! HA! THERE'S NOT MUCH THE MATTER WITH YOU! THOUGH I DO BELIEVE THAT IF YOU WERE ON YOUR DEATHBED YOU'D MAKE A JOKE!"
Irrepressible Patient: "WHY, OF COURSE I SHOULD. IT WOULD BE MY LAST CHANCE!"

Johnny (who has to face a bad Monday, to Manager of Messrs. R-thsch-ld's): "AH! I — WANT — O — AH! SEE YOU ABOUT AN OVERDRAFT."
Manager: "HOW MUCH DO YOU REQUIRE?"
Johnny: "AH! — HOW MUCH HAVE YOU GOT?"

Publisher (impatiently): "WELL, SIR, WHAT IS IT?" *Poet (timidly):* "O — ER — ARE YOU MR JOBSON?" *Publisher (irritably):* "YES." *Poet (more timidly):* "MR GEORGE JOBSON?" *Publisher (excitably):* "YES, SIR, THAT'S MY NAME." *Poet (more timidly still):* "OF THE FIRM OF MESSRS JOBSON AND DOODLE?" *Publisher (angrily):* "YES. WHAT DO YOU WANT?" *Poet:* "OH — I WANT TO SEE MR DOODLE!"

bowling away to Notting Hill, Brunswick or Kensington, chasing up his weekly cartoon." Evidently Burnand was a little wary of his new addition to the fold, noticing a certain similarity in temperament to John Leech, and indeed the amiable May gave Burnand some hair-raising moments. He once sent in a sketch right at the last minute, just before press time. It was a tiny drawing of a fat boy pulling the cork out of a wine bottle, with the quip: "Herewith my full page drawing, as promised."

Like a tiresome schoolboy, Phil May was often hauled up before Francis Burnand for some outrage or other. Once when summoned to the editorial sanctum he found Burnand occupied and likely to be engaged for at least half an hour. It gave him time to resort to a ploy. Hansoms were available at the office door, with a number of theatrical costumiers within a few minutes' drive. With this knowledge, Phil made good use of his time. When he returned, he tapped timidly on the editor's door and made his entrance. The furious Burnand turned round to find his penitent artist transformed into a forlorn Little Lord Fauntleroy, dressed pathetically in black velvet with a lace collar and white socks. The intended editorial reproof dissolved into a roar of laughter.

Fellow *Punch* contributor Lawrence Bradbury had another story to illustrate Phil May's irrepressible character. May would frequently visit Bradbury's home at Cranbrook in Kent, where, on one occasion, his genial host pressured him into a game of cricket. Phil was never a keen sportsman, though willing to make up numbers if called upon. The match was a village green affair; Bradbury's side were batting. Duly arrayed in pads and gloves, Phil had a bat thrust into his hands. Having received hurried instructions to hit the ball and run like mad, he marched off to the crease. Bradbury's team were in trouble with only one batsman of any note left at the other end of the wicket, but if Phil could stop with him there was still a chance. The first ball came thundering down at Phil and he hit it a yard or two in front of him — clearly excellent, but it gave no chance for a run. However, Phil had had his instructions and the dismayed batsman at the other end watched helplessly as Phil galloped wildly down the pitch. He did what he could to comply with May's call, but was run out by yards.

Phil's ignorance of the niceties of cricket was further demonstrated in one of the drawings he did for a famous series called "The Labours of 'Arry". This showed a square leg fieldsman mysteriously wearing wicket keeper's gloves. It worried W. G. Grace so much that the great cricketer sent May a telegram: "WHY, OH WHY, DOES SQUARE LEG WEAR WICKET KEEPING GLOVES?" The query appeared before Phil one evening at dinner, though he waited until long after his meal before he sent W. G. a reply. It was very late by the time it was handed to the great man, who had to be roused from his bed to receive the important communiqué: "TO KEEP HIS HANDS WARM."

Despite his lack of sporting talent, Phil May adopted a "sporty" style of dress which became well known in London. To keep up with this image, he bought himself a new horse, appropriately named Punch, which was to suffer the same fate as its predecessor. One night Phil left him in the charge of a loafer outside the National Sporting Club and later drove home in his customary hansom, only to remember Punch next morning. On another occasion he called on Bernard Partridge who was breakfasting with friends in his garden. Punch was brought into the grounds and grazed quietly on Partridge's flower beds while Phil joined the party and merrily chatted through breakfast. After he had left, Forbes-Robertson, the actor, who should have recognised Phil from his distinctive style

"THE TWELVE LABOURS OF 'ARRY"
FIFTH LABOUR — 'ARRY AT GOLF

of dress, turned to Partridge and enquired: "Who *was* that extraordinary character?"

Bernard Partridge and May had much in common. Both hankered after the stage and were ardent theatre-goers. Partridge even adopted the title of "Artist and Actor". Early in his career he had played Laertes to Forbes-Robertson's Hamlet, acting under the *nom-de-théâtre* of Bernard Gould; he also appeared in Shaw's first performance of *Arms and the Man*. May took one final stab at acting when announcements appeared in the press in 1902 that he was to take the part of Pistol in William Mollison's production of *Henry V*. Mollison described him as having "a fine conception of the part, a delicious sense of humour and an eccentric style that would have made any audience roar with laughter" but unfortunately the venture came to nothing as Phil May never appeared at rehearsals.

Partridge had joined the staff of *Punch* in 1891, before Phil May, and in 1901 he was appointed second cartoonist to Linley Sambourne. His career with *Punch* was long and distinguished. Before he became Sir Bernard he was noted for his hilarious repertoire of "Taking Phil May home" stories. He was a reliable accomplice: if Phil missed the weekly *Punch* dinner for his usual reason Partridge would pocket a menu card for him to take back to Lilian as evidence of an evening profitably spent. Partridge and May moved in the same circles and both frequented Romano's.

Phil May influenced Partridge deeply, though these two *Punch* cartoonists complemented each other in style as well as temperament. Partridge's pen was a sabre to Phil May's rapier, while Sambourne's broadsword completed the armoury. *Punch* had already given the word "cartoon" its present meaning (Leech and Tenniel were responsible for that), but May's contribution to posterity was more devastating. He established a method of pictorial shorthand which was to affect cartoonists right up to the present time. In a sense Phil May continued where Charles Keene, another brilliant *Punch* artist who had died in 1891, had left off. Keene, unlike May, was a withdrawn character, but he shared May's bohemian tastes. He found inspiration in workhouses and alleyways where fellow artists such as Du Maurier were not to be seen. An enthusiast for Keene's work was Lord Leighton, the august President of the Royal Academy.

Among the many aspiring cartoonists of the 'nineties was the Scottish artist George Armour, who became well known for the sporting subjects he contributed to *Punch*. He was exactly the same age as Phil May, and modelled his style on May's, though his drawings were never able to achieve the same impact. Though he could not be faulted in his drawing of horses, his style lacked individuality, being very similar to that of Raven-Hill. He remained a regular contributor to *Punch* throughout his life. Armour was doubtless gifted with powers of astute observation. In his autobiography, *Bridle and Brush*, he described Phil May:

Those who knew Phil May only in his down-town mood, if it can be so called, did not know the real nature of the man. I have heard him, when quietly at home, read or repeat some little bit of quite serious verse, as I should be glad to be able to do; also, though almost without voice, sing a serious song in a way that showed he appreciated every part of it.

He also recalled two of Phil May's favourite sayings: "Everyone's a good fellow till you know him," and "If I'd all the money I've lent, I'd be a rich man."

Jinks: "I WANT TO BUY A DOG. I DON'T KNOW WHAT THEY CALL THE BREED, BUT IT IS SOMETHING THE SHAPE OF A GREYHOUND, WITH A SHORT, CURLY TAIL AND ROUGH HAIR. DO YOU KEEP DOGS LIKE THAT?"

Fancier: "NO, I DROWNS 'EM!"

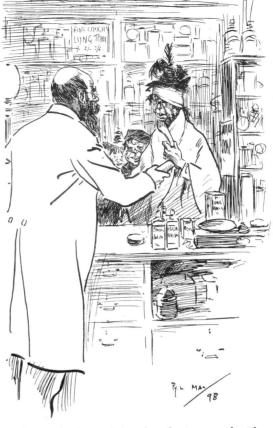

Chemist (to battered female, who is covered with scratches): "THE CAT, I SUPPOSE?"

Battered Female: "NO. ANUVVER LYDY!"

Irate Individual: "CONFOUND IT, WAITER, DIDN'T I TELL YOU I WAS IN A HURRY, AND ONLY WANTED ONE EGG?" WHY THE DICKENS DID YOU BRING ME *TWO*?"

Waiter (rather hurt): "I THOUGHT, AS YOU WAS IN A HURRY, SIR, I'D BRING TWO, 'COS ONE OF 'EM MIGHT BE BAD!"

"WHO PAYS THE PIPER CALLS THE TUNE"

Johnnie (to waiter): "AW — YOU'RE THE BOSS — HEAD WAITER, EH?"

Waiter: "YESSIR."

Johnnie: "AH WELL, JUST — AH — SEND UP TO YOUR *ORCHESTRA CHAPS*, AND TELL 'EM I REALLY CAN'T EAT MY DINNER TO *THAT* TUNE."

At 'Appy 'Ampstead on Easter Monday
A good example of Phil May's economy and strength of line
From "Phil May's Sketch-book"

It was May who persuaded Armour to keep sending his contributions to *Punch* and he saw to it that they reached Burnand's desk. Armour was not by any means the only person whom Phil May helped; he got many new artists their first chance. After his own early difficulties he no doubt felt that everyone deserved at least one break. Perhaps this explains the proliferation of May-orientated cartoonists in the pages on *Punch* during the early years of this century. Reynolds, Thorpe, Raven-Hill, Thomas and Shepherd, as well as Armour, all acknowledged Phil May's kindness and genius.

Amidst the many apochryphal Phil May stories which circulated were two which are well substantiated. One concerned a Chinese giant called Chang, a circus performer whom Phil was commissioned to make a sketch of. At the sitting he asked Chang to place his huge hand flat upon the page of his sketch book. Phil carefully traced round it till he came to the thumb. "That'll make two columns," he mused (he was paid by the column). "Here, Chang, put out your thumb. Another column!"

The second story, which concerned Phil May's time in Australia, working for the Sydney *Bulletin* was recalled by George Armour in *Bridle and Brush*:

> Phil had been away somewhere, but returned to Sydney on receipt of a telegram from the paper asking him to attend the first night of a play. He arrived just in time to go to the theatre, without calling at the hotel where his wife lived. After the play followed some kind of celebration supper to the players, in which Phil, of course, joined. This made the time of getting home very late, so, not wishing to awaken his wife, he went in without a light, undressed and crept into bed. Waking when daylight began to come, he turned over to find to his horror that the person occupying the bed with him was not Mrs May, but an intimate friend of hers, a lady who, like himself, was on the staff of the *Bulletin*, and had been called back to town, as he had, to attend the first night. Phil's description of how he crept out of bed, inch by inch, gathered his clothes and opened the door a hair's-breadth at a time, dreading the slightest creak, dressed on the landing, and stole away, was a masterpiece of dramatic description. All went well, however, and the explanation turned out to be that, in Phil's absence, Lilian had been staying with another friend out of town, and, unaware that Phil had been recalled, she had told her journalist friend to use the unoccupied room. He did not say if the lady in question was ever told of the incident.

The subject of humorous art in England is an interesting one. Usually there is a clear line between art and humour, but certain artists, from Hogarth to Rowlandson and Gillray, and the more recent contributors to *Punch* were able to combine them in a way that was frequently memorable, though many jokes soon die and only the best have stood the test of time. Much in Hogarth and Rowlandson has lost its bite, though Gillray has survived particularly well, as indeed has Phil May. May was a perfect recorder of late Victorian society, "an imp in a social teacup". He appeared at a time when the art of illustration reached its peak, and was well in the forefront. Though in terms of celebrity he was not the most important of artists, never having, for instance, received a knighthood or other honour, his contribution to humorous art was devastating. He outstripped such contemporaries as Tenniel, Sambourne, Partridge and Du Maurier. Even the most commercial of other artists really wanted to be "hung on the line" at the Royal Academy, but with May it was different. To him drawing was a mere means to an end: it paid for the booze. In the circumstances it was somewhat surprising that Lord Leighton contemplated proposing Phil May, whom he greatly admired, for election as an Associate of the Royal

SHOW SUNDAY

Brown (trying to find something to admire in Smudge's painting): "By Jove, old chap, those flowers are beautifully put in!"
Smudge: "Yes; my old friend — Thingummy — 'R.A.' you know, painted them in for me."

Academy. Such an appointment would have been a revolutionary step for the staid Academy, and after Leighton's death in 1896 no other Academician had the temerity to adopt the proposal.

Before Leighton's time no Royal Academician would seriously have considered the likes of Leech, Doyle or Tenniel fine artists: they were simply illustrators. There was a clear-cut distinction. Leighton was in some measure to change this attitude towards the art of illustration in the last year of his presidency, when were elected Solomon J. Solomon and Edwin Abbey, both extremely competent illustrators. In this light his proposal of Phil May has greater credibility. This was a time when there was a great emphasis on the technical skill of draughtsmanship.

In Phil May's drawings the artist, the man and the humorist are one. A great many of his jokes were drawn from observation rather than imagination, and many had an autobiographical theme. He once told his brother that he wished to follow Hogarth in recording the mannerisms and foibles of his day. This he achieved to a far greater degree than did any of his contemporaries.

IN THE ARTIST'S ROOM

Potztausand: "MY FRIEND, IT IS KOLASSAL!" MOST REMARK-WORTHY! YOU REMIND ME ON RUBINSTEIN; BUT YOU ARE BETTER AS HE."
Pianist (pleased): "INDEED! HOW?"
Potztausand: "IN DE BERSBIRATION. MY FRIEND RUBINSTEIN COULD NEVER BERSPIRE SO MOCH!"

BROTHERS IN ART

New Arrival: "WHAT SHOULD I CHARGE FOR TEACHING ZE PIANOFORTE?"
Old Stager: "OH, I DON'T KNOW."
New Arrival: "VELL, TELL ME VOT *YOU* CHARGE."
Old Stager: "I CHARGE FIVE GUINEAS A LESSON."
New Arrival: "HIMMEL! HOW MANY PUPILS HAVE YOU GOT?"
Old Stager: "OH, I HAVE NO PUPILS!"

LEAP-FROG

SHUTTLE COCK

PLAYING AT HORSES.

A GAME AT BALL.

From "Guttersnipes"

80

7 Rowsley House

HE ACCOLADE of Phil May's election to *Punch* was to be resoundingly
justified in 1896 with the publication of *Guttersnipes*, which set the seal of
fame on his career. If Oscar Wilde was to be remembered by his trials,
which had taken place the previous year, Phil May achieved immortality
with his *Guttersnipes*, a collection of fifty true-to-life pen drawings of Victorian low-
life children, their pranks and games. The book received rave reviews in the press.
There was "genius in every page" acclaimed *The Star*, while *The Observer* soberly
assured its readers that it "should be in much demand as a gift book". To *The Bath
Herald* it was "a masterpiece of humour" — and so it was. The first impression of
one thousand and fifty copies was quickly sold and the book was reprinted in a
cheaper three-and-sixpenny edition to meet demand.

May's guttersnipes were commonly supposed to have been inspired directly by
London's East End: after all, he spent much of his time drawing Cockney coster-
mongers and washerwomen. But they went back further than that: they were
drawn from memories of his own childhood in Leeds. Based on old friends and
accomplices, the faces of his little urchins have an almost ghost-like quality. Behind
them were traced the mud banks of Wapping or the backstreets of Hackney, but his
characters themselves are universal. On an historical level, the series is a fascinating
record of the lives of many a real urchin in the late nineteenth century. May seems
to have a great rapport with them: "I was a *Guttersnipe* myself once!" he confessed.

May would frequently use his friends, instead of professional models, as subjects,
and even the face of Phil May himself appears in his crowds, observing. There is a
hint of a more serious side to the *Guttersnipes* drawings which is reminiscent of the
quality of Goya's later drawings. The Spanish master was able to capture the very
truth of man's terrible cruelty to man in drawings that are frequently brutal and
harrowing. May, with his light comic touch, only borders on such revelations, but
the sense of foreboding is there. Unlike Goya, May was a kind caricaturist. He did
not delve into the grotesque, and he withheld moral judgements: his drawings ooze
charm and are as clean-cut and unpretentious as the day he put pen to paper.

May understood the tragedy of the slums only too well, his own tough up-
bringing having taught him exactly what they were like to live in. Friends called
him "the kindest and most generous soul imaginable". It was not unusual for May
to give a newspaper boy half a crown for an evening paper if he thought "the little
beggar looked as if he could do with a good meal", or, when he had no money on
him, give his gold watch or overcoat instead, instructing the recipient to get what
he could for it at the pawnshop and let him have the ticket. Phil's open-handedness
in buying drinks was well known, and even casual visitors to his studio came away
with pockets full of cigars. A friend once described a particular incident which
demonstrates his impetuous generosity.

A young girl of about sixteen went into a West End bar where Phil was leaning on the
counter, imbibing freely. He noticed that she was being pushed and shunted about as

'WHIP-BEHIND.'

TANTALIZING!

"ORRIBLE AND RE-VOLTIN' DETAILS, SIR!"

WHISTLING THE LAST
NEW TUNE.

From "Guttersnipes"

she was trying to sell her penny bunches of violets. Phil took pity on her and, seeing that her boots were in a sadly broken condition, stopped her and gave her a sovereign to get them mended. He instructed her to bring back the change and, taking her basket as security, he escorted her from the bar. As soon as her back was turned he cajoled his friends and everyone else in that crowded room to buy a bunch of violets. With a broad grin on his face and the cigar that never left his mouth, he blurted out: "Violets a bob!" When in due course the girl returned in her mended boots, she found herself in the presence of a barful of men wearing her violets and the quizzical looking man who had given her the sovereign handed her a basket empty of flowers but heavy with shillings. The kindness so overwhelmed her that she burst into tears.

The extra money brought in by *Guttersnipes* enabled the Mays to move to Rowsley House in Holland Park Road, which was only a few blocks from number 7. It was soon to become known as one of the most hospitable houses in London. Rowsley House had an impressive façade which, to the benefit of neighbours, was distinctive even to Phil's most drunken friends. The house at number 7 was part of a terrace in which all the houses looked alike, and there was not one of these occupants who had not been disturbed by a rumbustious caller knocking at the wrong door.

A third member of the May household who had made the move from number 7 to Rowsley House with them, was Gyp the terrier, the apple of Lilian's eye, who kept her company on many a long, lonely night when Phil was out. This friendly little soul had one unfortunate characteristic — a passion for hats. Many a guest had lost his topper when foolish enough to leave it unattended. It was not that Gyp, exactly, ate them; it was more a process of worrying them to death and then abandoning them in a helpless state of shreds and tatters. Lilian, well aware of her friend's strange predilection, was careful to keep her own millinery out of reach, though the less organised Phil suffered the loss of many a bowler. On one occasion Phil and Lilian were preparing to dine out — it was a white tie, tails and topper affair — when Phil recalled that his last respectable hat had been reduced by Gyp to a heap of demoralised shreds. He summoned the maid to hurry to the hatters just before closing, where half a dozen possible hats were piled into her arms: Mr May was to choose the one he wanted and send the other five back in the morning. Phil made his selection and he and Lilian departed for a pleasant evening among friends, where they enjoyed themselves thoroughly. They returned home after midnight to discover that Gyp, too, had had a most enjoyable evening — chewing up all five other hats!

Soon after the Mays moved to Rowsley House, poor Gyp died (perhaps due to a particularly venomous green bowler). After a suitable period of mourning, Phil bought Lilian another dog, which he called Mr Blathers because of its bulldog slavering and peculiar jowl movements. Mr Blathers looked very ferocious, but was harmless at heart, and one particular interviewer had no trouble getting past him. Phil was working in his studio at the time, trying to complete a drawing for *Punch*. The journalist was well known as a bore, and notoriously difficult to get rid of. His advent irritated Phil, immersed in sketching a costermonger at his usual rate of payment. The journalist was clearly not concerned about wasting valuable time. Phil needed a way to get rid of him. He invited him into the yard, where his costermonger model had left his cartload of vegetables. "Did you know," he asked the journalist, "if both ends are evenly balanced, this cart can be pulled as easily as if it were empty?" His victim looked suitably astounded. "If you'll just sit on the back for a minute," continued Phil, "and I get on the front, you'll see what I mean." The interviewer did as he was bade, perching on the back of the cart as Phil gingerly clambered into the front seat. He whipped the donkey, which dashed off with a jerk and the whole equipage careered into Kensington High Street, the disconcerted journalist clinging to the back. The barrow was excellently balanced for the best part of a quarter mile and amused many passers by until at last the donkey pulled up and the interviewer tumbled off the back, denting his top hat. The interview had come to an end.

In 1897 Phil May followed *Guttersnipes* with his *A.B.C.*, also published by the Leadenhall Press, and once again featuring dirty little ragamuffins. My own favourites among this selection are "Getting Father Home", "Getting Money for Father" and "Lost", the last perfectly crystallising that appalling moment when a very small person realises his parents are no longer with him and he is utterly alone.

Phil May's special love and understanding of children was demonstrated at a house party given by Sir Henry Lucy, to whose country estate Phil and Lilian had been invited for a weekend. Bored with the idle chat, Phil begged leave to retire and when he had not returned after a couple of hours Sir Henry went to look for him, only to discover him in the hallway with the children, down on his hands and knees giving them rides on his back.

"What on earth are you doing down there?" asked his host.

"I'm just enjoying myself," answered Phil with an air of surprise.

In the summer of 1897 Francis Burnand asked May to collaborate with him in producing a series called "Round and About the Beautiful and Bold Kentish Coast". Burnand was to provide the text, which May was to illustrate. Eventually these sketches were to be published in book form by A. & C. Black. When visited by the interviewer from the *Idler*, Phil sounded excited about this project: "By the way," he explained, "I have got something special in hand. We are writing a guide book to Kent. Of course I mean that I shall do the sketches and leave the writing part to Mr Burnand."

In the same interview, Phil enthused about horseriding over other modes of travel. "I much prefer my old gee-gee. He's thrown me off a dozen times, but I have come off without a scratch so far. Yes, my life is insured. It's my idea of saving money: if I die it reverts to the wife, it I don't — I mean, that is, before then, don't you know — it comes back to me when I'm fifty. Only eighteen years to wait for my accumulated savings." In fact, when Phil May died no such insurance policy was found. He went on to tell the interviewer: "No, I don't earn a hundred a day. Never did. Some idiot once printed that statement and I've been dunned right and left ever since. No, I don't turn out as much work as I used to, say three years ago, but the reason is that at that time I was freelance, and now I am retained specially by *Punch* and the *Graphic*. I can only do outside work by permission. Then, of course, there is my annual. I am three years ahead now — its circulation is indeed prodigious."

When Phil had finished his commission of the Kentish Coast book, he and Lilian went to Yorkshire for a week's holiday, visiting Lilian's parents and Phil's mother. Their coffers being much fuller now, one morning when Phil passed a tailor's shop in Leeds and remembered the suit he had ordered back in 1883 and never paid for, he obeyed his pricking conscience and rushed inside. "I want to pay for a suit."

Reference was made to ledgers dating back many years but no trace of the suit could be found. "Go on, keep looking," Phil insisted. "It's got to be in there somewhere." At last the proprietor was summoned, who immediately recognised his former, now famous, client, and was prepared to dismiss the subject of payment as a trifle. "I'm not going to leave this shop until I get a receipt!" said the benign Phil stubbornly.

Phil May and Lilian at home

Coster Girl

A Negress

A Chinaman

"A pin!"

Some of these chalk drawings were done as lightning sketches at smoking concerts

Details were given of what sort of suit it was and when it was bought, and Phil enquired how much the bill would be.

"Five pounds, Mr May."

"No fear," replied Phil, "I want discount for cash!"

The bemused tailor handed him a receipt dated November 6th 1897 for £4 10s.

In 1898 the *Graphic* sent Phil May to Holland, a trip which was to prove more profitable than the disastrous American fiasco. Instead of returning with a blank sketch book, he found inspiration among the dykes, windmills and cobbled streets of the Dutch landscape, and visited the Frans Hals museum at Haarlem. As a result, he began one of his most successful series, the "Volendam Suite", the sketches for which were completed in 1903 and published in the *Graphic*.

Phil May liked to build up his image as a travelled man, which went well with his carefully contrived sporty appearance, his check coats, well-cut breeches and shining leather gaiters. A contemporary with much the same taste in dress, though famous only within a select band of artists and writers, was the animal painter Joseph Crawhall, one of the most distinguished artists of the Glasgow School. Crawhall (1861-1913), whose excellent biography by Adrian Bury was published in 1958, had a profound effect on British watercolour painting. He was the son of Joseph Crawhall (1821-96) the illustrator (who provided Keene with many of his *Punch* jokes). Crawhall and May had a high opinion of each other's work, though their first meeting at the Savage Club had been engineered by Raven-Hill for a different reason: they so closely resembled one another in appearance. When they met, each stared at the other in speechless amazement.

Most of the foremost graphic artists of the 1890s worked in close proximity to each other. Their circle was small and somewhat elitist, but their influence was unquestionably profound. Together they had revolutionised graphic illustration, and as their importance became established, so did their social standing. Linley Sambourne held intimate Friday night gatherings for this little circle, where conversation flowed freely at his dinner table, and the Pennells offered similar soirées on Thursdays. Add to that the Mays' "at home on Sunday" tradition and the hectic club life, and there was little room left in anyone's social diary for anything else.

Elizabeth Robins Pennell in 1916 recalled her Thursday soirées. Describing herself as being "obsessed by my old fashioned notion as hostess that people could not enjoy themselves unless they were kept moving," she said she would flit about from guest to guest. Guests would include such famous men as Beardsley, Raven-Hill, Hartrick, E. J. Sullivan and, of course, Phil May. May and Beardsley, she noted, "were two of the artists who had most influence on black-and-white in the nineties", though, she added, "their art was poles apart". She recalls, with a refreshing candour of observation:

> Beardsley was fond of talk, always had something to say and was always eager to say it. All Phil May asked was not to be expected to say anything, to be allowed to smile amiably his dissent or approval. Had the rest of our company been of his mind in the matter, it would not have been so much easier for us to start the talk at once than to stop it at a reasonable hour, our Thursday nights would not have been so deafening with talk that I do not yet understand why the other tenants in the house did not unite in an indignant protest to the landlord.

It was not laziness that kept Phil May silent; speeches were just not his style. He was once asked to address a women's club at the Society of Arts, and

confronted the assembled crowd with a formidable looking manuscript in his hand. The speech had been written by a friend. "Far be it for me . . ." it began. That was as far as Phil got; he couldn't go on. Instead he spent the rest of his hour drawing on large sheets of paper and thus thoroughly amusing his audience. He said later of the speech: "I put it down because it just didn't sound like me, did it?"

Elizabeth Robins Pennell observed that Phil May was at his most voluble in the company of one or two people. She found it hard to define the secret of his immense popularity. "I do not know what the attraction was that made everybody like him," she wrote, "not merely the riffraff and the loafers who hung about his studio and waylaid him in the street for what they could get out of him, but all sorts of people who asked for nothing save his company — I could never define the attraction to myself. It was not his looks."

If Beardsley was the dandy of Piccadilly, May was the dandy of the racecourse, whose idiosyncratic horsey attire set something of a fashion among his admirers until they allowed it to degenerate into an affectation and the artist's velvet jacket, baggy corduroys and unkempt hair became hackneyed. Mrs Pennell added:

Neither his looks nor his silence, however original and personal, could have been the cause of the charm he undeniably possessed. I think he was one of the people whom one feels are nice instinctively, without any reason. He was sympathetic and responsive, serious when the occasion called for it, foolish when folly was in order. It wasn't only in his drawings that he was ready to wear the cap and bells. I know an artist, one of whose cherished memories of Phil May is of the Christmas Eve when they both rang Lord Leighton's door-bell and ran away and back to Phil May's studio on the other side of the road, and Phil May was as pleased as if it had been a masterpiece for *Punch*. He was naturally kind, amiable perhaps because it was the simplest thing to be. In his own house his amiability forced him to break his silence, but his remarks then, as far as I heard them, were usually confined to the monotonous offer, "Have a cigar!" "Have a whiskey-and-soda!" or "Have a drawing!" if anyone happened to express admiration for his work.

With her husband, the American artist Joseph, the authoress Mrs Pennell frequently attended the Mays' "open house", where Phil chatted more freely on his home ground, though he was always nervous in company when sober — which no doubt partly explained why he drank so much. Elizabeth Robins Pennell described him as an "ugly, delightful, smiling man, with a devoted band of admirers around him", the two most faithful of which were Hartrick and Sullivan who "were never far away". If anyone tried to lure either away from Phil, they succeeded only briefly. Their greatest joy was to talk shop to him. These two young artists were candidly enthusiastic about May's genius, and were both no doubt very fond of him in personal terms. They would often stay late at the Pennells on Thursdays to watch over him — and he did of course need some watching: at that time of the morning Phil would have given anything to anyone.

At home, undisturbed by friends or hangers-on, Phil May was a quiet, studious man, a sentimental man who would accumulate mementoes for their memories rather than monetary value. His artistic output was of course prolific and when left to himself in working mood he could produce drawings with immense speed.

The furnishings of Rowsley House were unostentatious. There were a few Persian rugs — normal enough in a Victorian home — and a carved Indian table; for the rest there was little of great value. The paintings on the walls were by friends. It was a cheerful house. Mr Blathers, the bulldog, guarded the door while the caged canary sang incessantly, and Lilian kept a discreet eye on their few possessions. Augustus Moore once described the studio in Rowsley House:

> The mantelpiece is peopled with little Japanese dolls, little bronzes and brasses and figures carved in yellow ivory. These, with a few plaster casts of arms and legs which hang on the walls, a line of Japanese prints put around the ceiling "to try an effect", a few Japanese lanterns hanging from the roof, some Japanese lay-figures in armour standing round the walls, and a few sketches, are about all the decoration of this long sky-lit room.

Phil May's drawing board, Moore also noted, looked like an address book with all the names scribbled on it, while the old grandfather clock which stood by the fireplace had given up the ghost, repeating, "For ever, never!"

"AN ENGLISHMAN'S HOUSE" &c

Maid (looking over wall to newly-married couple just returned from their honeymoon): "OH, PLEASE 'M, THAT DOG WAS SENT HERE YESTERDAY AS A WEDDING PRESENT; AND NONE OF US CAN'T GO NEAR HIM. YOU'LL HAVE TO COME IN BY THE BACK WAY!"

Brown (who has been dining at the Club with Jones): "JUST COME IN A MINUTE, OLD FELLOW, AND HAVE A NIGHTCAP."
Jones: "I'M AFRAID IT'S GETTING LATE. LET'S SEE HOW'S THE ENEMY."
Brown: "OH! THAT'S ALL RIGHT. *SHE'S* IN BED."

8 Bohemian London

ALTHOUGH the music-halls have now vanished, with the costers and flower girls, in Phil May's time they were in their heyday, and packed every night. Little Tich and Marie Lloyd lit up their stages with a warm-hearted glow. In the theatre Gilbert and Sullivan strummed away with a series of hit musicals — *The Mikado, H.M.S. Pinafore, Iolanthe* — while, on the more serious stage, the great George Alexander was strutting about like a peacock and Forbes-Robertson running through Shakespeare. It was a time of adolescent actor-worship, when the world seemed full of embryo Irvings, Terrisses and Trees. In the streets of London the "all 'ot" man peddled his wares such as floury, mammoth earth-apples, buttery and 'ot. Queen Victoria was an institution on the throne, while Gladstone had made his final speech as Prime Minister on March 2nd 1894.

Phil May was not short of subject matter. He recorded a rollicking, bustling London which, from the Portobello Road to "'Appy 'Ampstead" and beyond was a juxtaposition of destitution and unabashed affluence. He was much concerned with class barriers and himself felt completely at home with street merchants who brought up large families on paltry wages, and with little guttersnipes and mudlarks who clamoured to earn the odd farthing in any way they could. Phil observed the paraffin vendor who sauntered along with the cry, "Pen pain!" — or a penn'orth of paraffin ("bottled sunlight" as it was called) — and once asked him how he came by his job.

"It's this 'ere way, sir — if y'er a straight 'un yer can do like me," explained the man. "Fust, yer borrows a barrer on the strength of yer 'onesty, then yer goes to the oil dealer and gets tick on the strength of yer barrer!"

In the days of the hansom, the brewer's dray and the open-topped omnibus which ran from Bank to Charing Cross, the din of London's streets must have been no less than it is today. Phil May would usually spend his lunchtimes in a nearby pub: in London the correct duration of lunch was generally reckoned to be half an hour — in Paris it was more likely to be two hours, but then all sorts of disreputable things, such as gambling, were permissible there which would be frowned on in staider London. But there was plenty of gaiety in turn-of-the-century London, where spats were now "in", and gaiters were "out", and where, within the sound of Bow Bells, a Cockney conversation (imagined by Phil May) might have run like this:

"I'm so ravernous 'ungry that I could eat an 'edge 'og ... and orful nice they are! The're better 'an bloaters!"

"Oh, you'd eat anyfink ... on'y gypsies eats 'edge 'ogs."

The Victorian middle-class looked down its nose on the working-class, dismissing its members as drunken, immoral loafers whose habits and language deserved disdain. Pietistic magazines such as *The Quiver* reported on missionary work by such bodies as the London City Mission, Open Air Mission or Church Army in the East End, where the Cockney dregs needed to be saved from their

Fussy Old Lady: "Now *don't* forget, Conductor.
I *want the Bank of England.*"
Conductor: "All right, Mum." (*Aside:*) "She *don't*
want *much*, do she, Mate?"

Passenger (rising politely): "Excuse me, Mum, but
. do you believe in Woman's Rights?"
New Woman: "Most certainly I do."
Passenger (resuming seat): "Oh well, then, stand
up for 'em!"

EASTER MONDAY

'Arry: "Do you pass any pubs on the way to Broad-
stairs, Cabby?"
Cabby: "Yes. Lots."
'Arry: "Well, *don't!*"

*'Bus Driver (to Cabby, who is trying to lash his
horse into something like a trot):* "Wot's the
matter with 'im, Willum? 'E don't seem 'isself
this mornin'. I believe you've bin an' changed
'is milk!"

dreadful way of life. Whitechapel was notorious, and Hackney even worse. Phil May, however, did not despise these much maligned vagabonds: his own background gave him a point of contact with them.

Among the reading population, Dickens and Thackeray were the foremost authors at that time. May, who had long been an admirer of Dickens, in 1898 undertook to do a series of illustrations for an edition to be published by George Allen. In one of his sketch books there is the draft of a letter to Allen dated February 17th 1898:

> I have been very ill, though I am happy to say I am getting all right again. I am sorry to say I must ask you for a little more time as I have been to sick for the last six months to do any serious work, and, as I wish this work to be my very best, I want to feel quite fit before I turn it out... I am trying to get all my ordinary work finished off six months ahead so that I can sit down and have nothing else to do but *David Copperfield.*

Phil May was recovering from alcoholic poisoning. The commission had come at a bad time: had it been three or four years earlier, when he was completing so much good work, no doubt Fred Barnard's famous Dickens illustrations would have been rivalled. As it was, this scheme, like so many others, never reached fruition, although three preliminary sketches were made. The illustrations for a book of old songs which Bradbury & Agnew wished to publish unfortunately suffered the same fate, though a few delightful sketches were completed — six pages of "Widecombe Fair" and the title-page for "Harvest Home".

May was one of very few artists whose fame warranted the production of an annual gift book of his own. These became so popular that the idea soon proliferated and the market became flooded with a plethora of annuals during this period. Many were of little merit, but those of May retain their charm. The master of simplicity, who could claim, "I can't remember a time when I didn't draw," filled these books with his pearly kings, his 'Arrys and 'Arriets, his humour as clipped, quick and urbane as his drawings. Free from malice and snobbery, it could appeal to people from all walks of life. These boldly simple drawings were the very reverse of the intricate creations of Beardsley. May once commented to Raven-Hill, "All I know, I got from Sambourne," meaning his down-to-earth approach as much as his technique, though clearly only Phil May could have achieved the mastery of a Phil May sketch.

The first *Phil May Annual* was published by The London Central Publishing & Advertising Company in the summer of 1892. Between that date and 1905 sixteen issues were published, thirteen winter and three summer numbers. After the first issue, Walter Haddon, May's old friend from the *St Stephen's Review*, took over the publication of the next four, while Neville Beeman produced the 1896 and 1897 winter issues and Messrs Thacker & Company the remainder. In 1898 Francis Gribble of Thackers lengthened the page, which, according to James Thorpe, "spoilt the uniformity". Nevertheless, five thousand copies of the 1898 winter annual were sold.

The annuals were a personal triumph for May, giving him a greater freedom of expression and establishing his name as a household word. He enjoyed not being constricted by rigid editorial policies, and although many of the drawings in the annuals were reproduced from the dailies and weeklies to which he contributed, he had more independence. Gribble's one complaint was that he had much difficulty in extracting May's work on time. There were also many literary contributions in these annuals from such writers as H. G. Wells, Kenneth Grahame and Conan

Sir Henry Irving
Lightning sketch in chalk

Sir Henry Irving
as Mephistopheles
Sketch at a Savage
Club Dinner

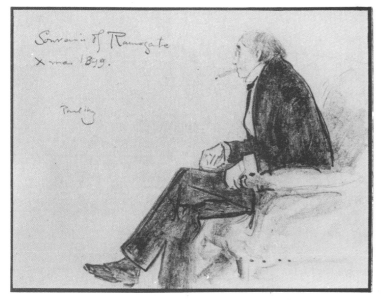

Another sketch of Sir Henry Irving
Drawn at one of Francis Burnand's
house-parties in Ramsgate

Famous Lion Comique (to his Agent, who is not much of a cigar smoker): "WHAT DID YOU THINK OF THAT CIGAR AS I GIVE YOU THE OTHER DAY?"
Agent: "WELL, THE FIRST NIGHT I LIKED IT WELL ENOUGH. BUT THE SECOND NIGHT I DIDN'T LIKE IT SO WELL. AND THE THIRD I DIDN'T LIKE IT AT ALL!"

THE GREAT PRIZE FIGHT

Johnnie (who finds that his Box, £20, has been appropriated by "the Fancy"): "I BEG YOUR PARDON, BUT THIS IS *MY* BOX!"
Bill Bashford: "OH, IS IT? WELL, WHY DON'T YOU TIKE IT?"

Conversationalist: "DO YOU PLAY PING-PONG?"
Actor: "NO. I PLAY *HAMLET!*"

THE NEW PLAY

Low Comedian: "HAVE YOU SEEN THE NOTICE?"
Tragedian: "NO; IS IT A GOOD ONE?"
Low Comedian: "IT'S A FORTNIGHT'S."

Doyle, who were at the beginning of their careers, and this combination of visual and verbal wit influenced the styling of the now defunct *Printers' Pie*.

The great actor Henry Irving, who so dominated the Victorian theatre, was a much admired friend of Phil May's. Irving achieved much acclaim in such plays as *The Bells, Richard III, The Lyons Mail* and *Becket*; he was undoubtedly a great actor, and, to his contemporaries, something infinitely more than an actor. When he stepped on to the stage, he seemed to radiate a mystical quality of aesthetic spirituality. He had the aura of a saint and the face of a scholar. Ellen Terry said of him:

> His soul was not more surely in his body than in the theatre. He thought of nothing else, cared for nothing else, went without his dinner to buy a book that might be helpful in studying, or a stage jewel that might be helpful to wear. He spent his life in incessant labour and denied himself everything for that purpose.

Although twenty-six years older than Phil May, Irving, whose real name was John Henry Brodribb, had something in common with May. He came from a yeoman family in Somerset and, like May, climbed the social ladder through sheer ability in his chosen vocation; Irving even achieved the final accolade of becoming the first British actor to be knighted. Like May, he had in his formative years sought his fortune in London, and nearly starved, his early privations telling later on his health. "It is strange how one never entirely makes up for not having had quite enough to eat in one's youth," he remarked. Irving was possessed of a magical magnetism as an established great actor and it would have been difficult for his later admirers to imagine him as an awkward boy in his teens, suffering the defects of a stutter, a limp and a general clumsiness that would have made an elephant look graceful. The determined Irving lived to overcome all these difficulties and become the darling of the Victorian theatre.

Between 1878, when Irving was offered the lease of the Lyceum, until 1896, he was something of a god. Ellen Terry, his leading lady, did much to help him keep his position of dominance. Even Queen Victoria is said to have admired Irving, breaking her usual silence to admit, "We are very, very pleased." It was only after 1896, when Irving became seriously ill for the first time in his life, that things started to go wrong. First, the Lyceum's entire stock of scenery, some 260 sets for forty-four plays, were destroyed in a fire: all the work they represented was wiped out in a single night. Secondly, there was the disastrous handing over of the financial responsibility for the Lyceum to a syndicate, and, finally, the passing of the directorship of the Lyceum from Irving into other hands. The worry of these setbacks was eventually to kill Irving. Nevertheless, a happy memory of Irving, in the form of a lightning sketch dashed off by Phil May, hangs in pride of place in the Savage Club.

Like Irving, Phil May enjoyed a good cigar — indeed a taste for a particular brand of expensive cigars, which cost him £10 or £12 a hundred (a high sum in those days) was the only personal extravagance of Phil's which Lilian seems to have begrudged him. Phil was seldom to be seen in public or private without a cigar in his mouth, and when Raven-Hill once called at his studio he was, with unusual diffidence, offered a highly decorated but otherwise doubtful cigar. As soon as they had left the house however, Phil threw away both cigars and led Raven-Hill into the private bar of a neighbouring tavern, where he had secreted a box of his own special brand. "Sorry to have given you that one, old man," he apologised quietly, "but Lil's got a sudden fit of economy."

Lilian would no doubt rather have spent on theatres or dinners the money which Phil lavished on his expensive cigars. They both enjoyed dining out. At one particular private dinner party at the Hotel Cecil which Phil and Lilian attended, the champagne and food were both good and abundant. When the ladies withdrew after dinner, Phil sank into a very low, deep armchair and lit up his usual cigar; the conversation turned to the subject of illustration, a favourite topic of Phil's. Inspired suddenly by a bright idea he needed to emphasise, he sprang forward, but his chair was so low and so deep that the plunge was a trifle uncontrolled. He fell head first on to the soft carpet, turned completely head over heels with the cigar still between his teeth, and ended up seated on the floor. He took one puff from his cigar and remarked, "I haven't done a somersault like that since I was a kid."

Phil's generosity to every parasite who pursued him, "actors" who had never been on the stage, "journalists" who had been kicked out of every office in Fleet Street, and "sportsmen" who were well known to the police, meant that he frequently found himself short of ready cash. On one occasion he gave a lunch for a party of friends at Romano's, the star item on the menu being a very special and expensive fruit salad. Phil's bill came to £35. Fortunately he had an arrangement with the publishers of his Annual that he should be paid £12 10s in cash for every drawing delivered, so he sent a messenger with a note begging, "Please hand the bearer £37 10s. The three drawings will be handed to you personally tomorrow." The money arrived within half an hour and the bill was paid; and the three drawings were duly delivered the next day.

Another in the lengthy literature of Phil May stories also concerned Romano's, though fortunately this incident did not cost Phil quite so much as his lunch party. With a group of friends round Romano's bar one night, the subject of conversation turned to last trains and the friends began comparing watches, which all differed. It was proposed that they should settle the precise time by going outside to look at the Law Courts clock. "Don't be silly," said Phil, remembering the two intervening churches, "you can't see it from here."

"I'll bet you a quid you can," answered the first man.

"Done!" replied Phil promptly, and the party trooped out into the Strand.

Sure enough, there was the clock, pointing plainly to ten minutes to twelve. Phil paid up and made a mental note of the curious fact.

A little later Romano himself appeared on the scene, and May skilfully led the conversation with him round to the accuracy of the bar clock, which, he was prepared to wager, differed from that at the Law Courts. The Roman fell easily into the trap and bet a sovereign that the clock could not be seen.

"Now then, my lad, come and have a look," said the triumphant Phil, and out they went. But, alas, no clock was visible. Phil began to wonder, as he parted with his second forfeit, whether he had been seeing things. There was a simple explanation, however: the light in the clock always went out at midnight.

London of the 'nineties belonged to Whistler: he had been involved in a famous lawsuit with Ruskin in 1878 (being awarded a farthing damages), but had emerged from it as an all the more spectacular figure. To Phil May in his formative years, Whistler was a paragon; his Venetian etchings exhibited in 1880 were only one side of this controversial and versatile artist's genius. Whistler was almost above fashion, and his fiercely independent temperament, not to say arrogance, appealed to May. The two men met infrequently, but Whistler was happy to propose Phil  May to the Chelsea Arts Club, where May's letter of thanks still hangs in the billiard-room. The Chelsea Arts Club was founded in 1889 as a haven of good food and relaxation for professional artists. Its first premises were in the Kings Road, on the site today occupied by the Chenil Galleries. Whistler and Sargent were among its original members, and Phil May was no doubt delighted to make one of this famous company. Edwin Ward recorded in *Recollections of a Savage*:

What a fascinating companion Phil was! I remember meeting him in the Chelsea Arts Club, then located in temporary premises at Jimmie Christie's lodgings in the Kings Road. It was a great evening, but — "Tell it not in Gath" — we found such comfort in each other's company that we forgot to "go home till morning". This made the succeeding day dull and difficult by comparison, but it was worth it and I am glad we did it. It was broad daylight when returning home dead tired and dropping with sleep, I softly tip-toed up the stairs to find the bedroom door ajar and — much to my relief — a small flicker of gas was evidence that my dear wife had slept peacefully through the night.

Superior 'Arry: "Cabby! To the — aw — Prince of Wales's."
Cabby: "Marlbro' 'Ouse, my Lord?"

97

It may not have passed unnoticed that such behaviour was normal practice with Phil May himself. Reports of these all-night sessions were substantiated by Mrs Rosa Lewis and Starr Wood. The former, better known as "The Duchess of Duke Street", was a close friend of King Edward VII and proprietor of the old Cavendish Hotel. After her death, one of May's sketches, executed on a tablecloth, was framed and sold among her effects: it was a cartoon advertising a brand of whisky, and was signed and dated 1902.

Starr Wood, who had rebelled against family pressures to make him an accountant and chosen instead the precarious world of Art, contributed to many periodicals, including *Fun, Judy* and *Moonshine*. He started his own magazine, *Windmill*, which lasted only a year or two, but almost a decade later had more success with his *Snarks' Annual*. He also produced a clever collection of caricatures and limericks under the title, *Rhymes of the Regiments*, though his subjects generally lay in the field of marital contretemps and domestic quirks. Starr Wood was a good friend of Phil May (he produced a parody pastiche of May's lightning sketch of Henry Irving in postcard form) and ended many an evening seeing Phil home.

Perhaps the best compliment Phil May ever received came from Whistler himself, when an interviewer asked him: "And now, Mr Whistler, what about black-and-white art?"

"Black-and-white art," said Whistler, "is summed up in two words — Phil May."

He elaborated on his views in a letter to *The Art Journal*: "I take a great delight in Phil May. Certainly his work interests me more than that of any man since Charles Keene — from whom he is quite distinct. There is a lightness and a daintiness in what he does combined with knowledge and wit, which singles him out from his contemporaries."

It was possibly Whistler's approbation which opened the door to the world of fine art to Phil May: in 1897 he was elected to the Royal Institute of Painters in Watercolours. It was his one and only honour. He was one of fourteen new members to be elected in that year (Dudley Hardy was another) and it entitled him to use the letters R.I. after his name, though, in typical May fashion, he frequently "forgot".

Whistler was particularly impressed by Phil May's "The Parson and the Painter" series, his little joke being to see Rothenstein, whose academic stuffiness he disliked, as the parson. Although Whistler heaped generous praise on May's drawings, Rothenstein refused to rank them in the same class as Charles Keene's.

As has already been noticed, Phil May was as casual about money as he was over the question of honours, treating both with complete disinterest. When delivering drawings he would insist on cash rather than a cheque, cash being so much more negotiable. When he had money on him, he carried it loose in his pockets or, sometimes, in his socks. Cab-touts, drivers, hall porters and commissionaires, like his flock of hangers on, all benefited from his largesse. Reichardt, the proprietor of *Pick-Me-Up*, once paid him £25 for some work, which had all disappeared by the time he reached home. Poor Lilian struggled unsuccessfully to manage the family  finances against disastrous odds. Once when it was necessary for Phil to entertain some business acquaintances, she advanced him a mere £4 in the hope that he would try for once to keep his expenses to a minimum. On his way to the dinner, however, he collected an additional £25 from Clement Shorter, the editor of the *Sketch*. In the course of the evening he spent everything, with the exception of £1, which was produced triumphantly next morning in exchange for Lilian's praise for his carefulness.

"I'M SURPRISED TO FIND THAT YOU KEEP A DOG,
TOMKINS! WHY, YOU CAN BARELY KEEP YOUR WIFE!
WHAT ON EARTH DO YOU FEED HIM ON?"
"WELL, I GIVES 'IM CAT'S-MEAT. AND WHEN I CAN'T
AFFORD THAT, WHY, 'E 'AS TO 'AVE WOT WE 'AVE."

*Diminutive Nursemaid (to Angler, who has not had
a bite for hours):* "OH, PLEASE, SIR, *DO* LET BABY
SEE YOU CATCH A FISH!"

*Charitable Person (who has been much impressed
by the erudition of a plausible cadger):* "YOU
SEEM TO BE A VERY WELL-INFORMED PERSON. WHERE
WERE YOU BROUGHT UP?"
Absent-minded Cadger (promptly): "AT BOW STREET,
PRINCIPALLY!"

Wretched-looking Messenger: "BEG PARDON, MR
BROWN, IT'S COME AT LARST! I'M *ENTIRELY* DEPEND-
ENT ON MYSELF. MY WIFE'S BEEN AND GOT A
SEPARATION ORDER!"

Street Serio (singing): "ER—YEW WILL THINK HOV ME AND LOVE ME HAS IN DIES HOV LONG AGO-O-O!"

OVERHEARD AT A COUNTRY FAIR

"'ERE Y' ARE! ALL THE JOLLY FUN! LYDIES' TORMENTORS TWO A PENNY!"

Mrs Snobson (who is doing a little slumming for the first time and wishes to appear affable, but is at a loss to know how to commence conversation): "TOWN VERY EMPTY!"

Q.E.D.

"WHAT'S UP WI' SAL?"
"AINT YER 'ERD? SHE'S MARRIED AGIN!"

May once admitted to A. S. Hartrick, in a mood of self-deprecatory remorse: "My father was a drunkard and I'm a drunkard." That was another reason why, despite his fame and success, May remained comparatively poor to the very end. In 1900, after more than ten years of regular and successful work, he still needed to borrow money to back one of the "dead certs" which the whispering gallery of Romano's circulated before every major race. Once Phil and A. E. Bumpstead ("the Pitcher") from the *Sporting Times* were tipped Oban for the Lincolnshire Handicap. They sent out urgent appeals for funds to friends and backed the horse with almost all they could lay their hands on, reserving only sufficient money to take them to the racecourse and buy them drinks until the bookies paid out.

Oban, however, did not oblige. Shortly before 11 p.m. the two friends arrived back in London, with just enough money to cover the cab fare to the Strand. In the cab Phil became slightly fidgety.

"What's the matter?" asked the Pitcher. "I mean over and above the treachery of Oban?"

"Can't go to the Roman's," answered Phil disconsolately. "I'm over the hilt."

The matter was very serious. The Pitcher himself was near enough the hilt to meet with opposition if he attempted to chalk up enough to cover them both. The cab pulled up outside Romano's and the Pitcher handed the cabby their combined fortunes. The cab drove away, leaving the two pacing up and down, weighing up the possibilities. These were negligible. Kind-hearted head-waiter Otto had been dead some ten years. Romano's now had a manager, the suave Luigi Naintre, who looked with disfavour upon slate customers. There would be many friends inside, no doubt, but they could not be counted upon as being able to to accommodate passengers on their own bills. What were they to do?

Suddenly little Phil grabbed the tall Pitcher by the sleeve. "Come with me!" he cried. "We're saved!" And before the Pitcher knew what was happening to him, Phil had dragged him through the door of Romano's. Still more perturbed was the Pitcher when Phil began to order a meal and drinks for them.

"I hope you know what you are doing, Phil," he remarked as the waiter left their table.

Without a word, Phil picked up the menu card and began to scrawl on it. In a few seconds the Pitcher saw a horse appearing. In a few more seconds he knew it was Oban. Phil wrote, "O DAMN OBAN" under it, and signed it. The next moment he was standing on his chair.

"What am I bid for this excellent drawing of a horse?" he shouted into the restaurant. "Will someone give me a start with a guinea?"

There was no shortage of bidders, and very soon the price began to settle round the four guinea level. But Phil was just warming to his auctioneering act.

"Four guineas I'm bid, gentlemen, four guineas for Oban — the horse that positively ruined the poor Pitcher and myself! Surely we can do better than that?"

"Five!" shouted a voice.

"Five and a half!" retorted another.

"Halves be damned — make it six," demanded Phil.

"Six it is!"

"Lot number one going for six guineas. Going — "

"Seven!"

"Did I hear you bid seven, sir? Pitch, order another bottle, there's a good man. Going at seven — "

"Eight!"

"Eight? It's *yours* — that's all it's worth!"

9   The Clubman

CLUBLAND, as can be imagined, was Phil May's element. He enjoyed company of any sort and mixed easily with people from all walks of life. The diverse list of the many clubs he joined speaks for itself. One example was the You-Be-Quiet Club, the purpose of which was to soften exiled Yorkshiremen in London by means of excellent dinners and concerts. May was proud to be associated with Yorkshire and at the club met many old friends from his early days in Leeds. On one of their menu covers he once caricatured Sammy Fox, Archibald Ramsden and himself as the three musketeers, showing his strongly sentimental link with bygone days. Always nostalgic, he looked back on his formative years with affection. He gave the drawing to Ramsden, signing it "From your errand boy."

Another of Phil May's haunts was the Punch Bowl Club, started by Percy Wood who looked like something out of a Dickens novel. It served a selective clientèle of bohemians and personable rogues. In his youth Wood had been trained as a sculptor and, working at his chosen profession, he had later amassed a fortune of some £8,000. With all his savings, he had gone to Monte Carlo, intending to break the bank; unfortunately the bank broke Percy Wood, and he was forced to return to London a sadder and hopefully wiser man. Having tasted the delights of easy money, he decided to have another try at making it from the opposite side of the fence, and opened his own casino. It looked slightly out of place in the peaceful purlieus of Marylebone, but attracted a lot of customers. Qualified croupiers were engaged, with all the paraphernalia of a fully furnished roulette room: nothing was forgotten. You could wine and dine regardless of cost and, although a modest entrance fee was insisted upon, which then placed all the club's resources at the disposal of customers, the one golden rule of gaming institutions, that of not allowing credit, Percy Wood forgot. Players who won were paid in full but those who lost were allowed to run up insurmountable bills, with the result that the casino was duly forced to close. Next, Wood took over a photography shop in Regent Street, where he gradually built up a small circle of friends which was the beginning of the Punch Bowl Club.

Earlier events would suggest that Wood was something less than an acute businessman, and the Punch Bowl Club also suffered from a lack of firm control. Though some members paid their subscriptions, the majority did not. When the club found itself in financial difficulties, Wood treated this as a matter of course; if a brewer or wine merchant called at the door to demand settlement, there had to be an immediate whip-round among members present. Finally the bailiffs stepped in, however, and Wood was forced to move from Regent Street to new premises in Wells Street. During the move a new billiard table miraculously appeared, which no doubt had something to do with the fact that the removal had taken place at midnight. Things did not improve however: at one point funds became so low that banisters were wrenched from the staircase to be used as firewood.

At the end of each season, when most clubs closed for cleaning operations, the

First Convivial: "'Sh two o'clock! Wha'll er Misshus shay?"

Second Convivial: "Thash all ri'! Shay you bin wi' me—(*hic*)!"

A BIG ORDER

Stout Party (to waitress): "Put me on a pancake, please!"

Scientific and Nervous Visitor at Country Hotel: "I suppose there's no 'Ptomaine' in this pie?"

Waiter (quite equal to the occasion): "No, sir. We never puts that in unless specially ordered!"

Stout Party: "Now then, waiter, what have you got?"

Waiter: "Calves' brains, devilled kidneys, fried liver—"

Stout Party: "Here! Bother your complaints! Give me the *menoo*?"

Punch Bowl would follow suit, though not for cleaning — it was to give the dust ample time to settle. Percy Wood would lock up the premises and, bearing a tray of cheap trinkets, would tramp the countryside selling his wares — an unusual occupation, you might think, for the proprietor of a popular London haunt, but financial stringencies can drive even the proud to extremes. From village to village he would roam, leading a nomadic existence, sleeping where he could and supping as a knight of the road. When the season was about to begin, he would trudge back to London, unfasten the padlock on the door of the Punch Bowl Club and resume his rôle as patron. During the season he lived on the premises and, apart from his annual selling trips, rarely ventured outside the club. If he did, it was probably no further than the cabmen's shelter, where a succulent chop, steak or bacon and eggs could be bought at any time of day or night. It was nicknamed the Junior Turf and May's regular cabby whiled away many a long hour there too, waiting for his fare. Percy Wood was popular in the cab drivers' covey, partly because he almost always had a supply of the club's whisky hidden in the voluminous sidepockets of his coat, but also on account of his ability to entertain in conversation. Because of his generosity, whisky supplies eventually ran short, and Percy was forced to seek a loan to keep the bonhomie flowing — using the gold in his teeth as collateral.

One of Wood's innovations was to supply a private latch-key to each member of the club, enabling members to come and go as they pleased. This liberty was particularly appreciated by those less affluent "Bowlers" who used the club as a home from home.

Percy Wood, who was well aware of Phil May's generosity, once, during a pressing spell of debt, begged for the loan of £50. The obliging Phil turfed out all he could and gave Percy £25, apologising for not being able to raise the full amount. Some time later a fellow Bowler asked May why he had not recently been seen at the club. "Well, you see," he explained, "I can't really; I still owe Percy £25!"

After Wood's death, the Punch Bowl Club was disbanded and the London Sketch Club moved into its vacant rooms. This was yet another of Phil May's clubs and, as a founder member, he was obliged to serve on its first council. In organisation the London Sketch Club was rather like the Savage, though most of its members were commercial artists. As a member of the council, Phil May's signature was needed on the lease of the new Wells Street studio. Walter Churcher, the secretary, tracked him down and recorded:

> Phil was in his most elusive, Puckish mood, but at last I ran him to earth one Sunday morning at Cecil Aldin's studio, outside which I found a cabman, who asked me to inform "the gent inside wiv a fringe" that he had been waiting a solid hour. My advice to the cabby was not to worry but to go on waiting. Well, the elusive Phil, when faced with my demand for his famous signature, "stone-walled", urged his "well known Sabbatarian principles" and so on, but finally agreed on one condition — that the thing was done in style. So an historic tableau was thereupon staged. Phil impersonated King John signing Magna Carta; Cecil Aldin, as a baron, knelt with pen and parchment; Dudley Hardy, as another baron, armed with a fearsome weapon, was ready to "dot" King John should he show any further reticence about the autograph. Thus were the deed and Deed "done in style", as Phil had insisted. I believe, too, that after our drive home that cabby was able to congratulate himself on taking my advice and waiting for "the gent wiv the fringe". Phil was always generous.

Phil May was not a frequent visitor to the London Sketch Club, though on one occasion when he did put in an appearance, he greatly impressed Lionel Edwards

Clerk: "RETURN?"
Pat: "PHWAT FOR 'UD OI BE WANTIN' A RETURN TICKUT
WHEN OI'M HERE ALREADY?"

Mrs O'Brady: "SHURE I WANT TO BANK TWINTY POUNDS.
CAN I DRAW IT OUT QUICK IF I WANT IT?"
Postmaster: "INDADE, MRS O'BRADY, YOU CAN DRAW IT
OUT TOMORROW IF YOU GIVE ME A WAKE'S NOTICE!"

Father O'Flynn: "AND NOW, PAT MURPHY, IN THIS
SEASON OF LENT, WHAT IS IT YE'LL DO BY WAY OF
PENANCE?"
Pat Murphy: "SURE, THEN, I'LL—I'LL COME AN' HEAR
YOUR RIVERANCE PRAYCHE!"

"SURE, PAT, AND WHAT ARE YE WEARIN' YE'R COAT
BUTTONED UP LOIKE THAT ON A WARM DAY LOIKE
THIS?"
"FAITH, YE'R RIVERENCE, TO HOIDE THE SHIRT OI
HAVEN'T ON!"

SATURDAY TILL MONDAY

Condoling Friend (to recently bereaved Widower):
"IT MUST BE AWFULLY HARD TO LOSE ONE'S WIFE."
The Bereaved: "YES — IT'S ALMOST *IMPOSSIBLE*!"

"'SCUSE ME, MISS, BUT CAN YOU 'BLIGE ME WITH A
CLOVE? I GOT ER MEET ER MISSHUS, AN' I DON'T
WANT 'ER TO NOTISH ELLYTHING."

"GOOD MORNING, MISS VOSS."
"MY NAME IS NOT VOSS. IT NEVER VOSS AND NEVER
VILL BE!"

From "The Phil May Folio"

with the way he sketched directly with a pen: "the result was miraculous, and seemed the more remarkable for its economy of line." On the same evening he enthralled his audience with the pathetic tale of a model and her mother, leading up to a climax which was eagerly awaited by everyone, by now close to tears. It never came; Phil admitted: "Clean forgotten the punch line!"

It was Phil May who was largely responsible for the members' attitude towards speeches. If anyone looked as if he were about to make a speech, cards were held aloft proclaiming, "Chuck it!", "Rats!", "Drop it!" or "Dry up!" The most hardened would-be orator would be disconcerted. A writer calling himself "A Lay Member" reported an amusing spoof on speechmaking in *The Art Record* of May 11th 1901:

> Phil May once made a famous speech. He arose with great ceremony and, gravely taking out a pair of spectacles, adjusted them on his nose with much gravity. He then coughed, and paused while he placed a pair of pince-nez over his spectacles. Having done this, he coughed again, and looked around, then, taking out another pair of glasses, put them on also. The members now sat waiting anxiously. He beamed through his various spectacles, which he similarly placed over the others. This went on for some time, always opening his mouth to speak, and then pausing to put on another pair of spectacles, until he had no less than seven or eight pairs. Then he spoke at last. He said: "Tut-tut!" and sat down gravely.

Last but not least of Phil May's clubs was the Savage Club itself, founded in 1857. Phil May joined it in 1893, handing in two pages of signatures backing up his proposer and seconder, which clearly demonstrated his popularity among this group of artists, writers, actors and musicians. The Savage was May's favourite resort. Past members had included such giants of the graphic art world as George Cruikshank and Harry Furniss, while the endless supply of members from the ranks of popular actors included J. L. Toole, George Alexander and Lionel Brough. Many of the actor members had been boyhood idols of Phil and the failed actor turned artist now mixed freely with the awesome Sir Henry Irving, the glittering Tree and the talented Squire Bancroft.

Members of the Savage Club were generally on first name terms — Phil May being universally referred to as "Good old Phil". There was one exception, however, a little known actor called E. J. Odell, who had taken clown parts in many of Irving's productions. Something of a character, he had frequently been expelled from the club for his egoistic and rude manners. No-one dared call him by any other name than Mr Odell. He was mean, grasping and devious. If anyone asked his age, he would refuse to answer; if asked what his initials stood for he would loftily reply, "Eberneezer Jehosophat." Not only did he keep his past a mystery, but he was also a bad-tempered old bore who would frequently sneer at other people's stories, and he spent his time scrounging drinks and cigars. When the future George VI was invited to the club as a guest of honour, he unwittingly sat in Odell's chair. "How dare you, Sir! That's my chair," fumed Odell. The Duke of York simply got up, apologised and went off to the bar with the composure of a gentleman. Edward VII had been the first member of the Royal Family to become a "Brother Savage" back in 1882. His election, when Prince of Wales, had started a tradition which was continued by both Georges and other members of the Royal Family. In a sympathetic moment Edward VII was to nominate Odell for a place with Charterhouse, where the disagreeable old man died in 1928.

Yet, strangely, Odell was known world-wide from Madeira to South Africa. The first question one brother Savage would ask another was, "How is old Odell?" —

107

an odd topic, considering the club's many really distinguished members. Dr Symons Eccles even commissioned the portrait painter Edwin Ward to immortalise Odell on canvas. When the painting was finished Eccles proudly announced that it should hang in the Rogues' Gallery, beside other Savage Club members' portraits. Rising at one of their house dinners, he asked, "Brother Savages — will you accept this portrait of Odell to hang in our club?"

There were loud shouts of, "No!" from all corners of the room. Dr Eccles carried his gift away; it hung in his drawing-room for many years until retrieved by Edwin Ward and taken back to the club some time later.

A typical feature of a Savage Club evening was the entertainment which followed the house dinner. According to their forte, members would act, sing or perform mystifying conjuring tricks, and artists would produce lightning sketches. Phil May could dash off half a dozen heads in coloured chalk — including, of course, one of the chairman of the evening — in half an hour, and his achievement set a precedent. Tom Browne, John Hassall, Dudley Hardy and Cecil Aldin followed suit in their different styles and this artistic turn became an important feature of the evening's entertainment. As Aaron Watson said, in his history of the Savage Club, these artists were "among the most ready, as well as the most able, of the entertainers."

An Impromptu by Phil May

On June 9th 1899 the Savage held a special supper at which Mark Twain was guest of honour. During the course of the evening he autographed one of the menu cards, along with the famous Marconi. Twain enjoyed the Savage bonhomie so much that he later became a member and it was at a subsequent meal that he made his famous, often quoted, remark about Chaucer, Shakespeare and Milton being dead, "And I'm not feeling very well myself!" His trip to England was shrouded in a certain mystery so that one desperate editor from the United States who had lost patience in trying to discover Twain's whereabouts, sent a letter addressed, "Mark Train, God knows where! Try London." The letter found him and Twain studied the reference to God, noting that the other party might have been more appropriate. The next letter was addressed, "Mark Twain, The Devil knows where! Try London." This also found him.

Phil May, who admired Twain's art and wit, persuaded him to attend a *Punch*

HONEYMOONING IN PARIS

Mrs Jones: "AM I NOT AN EXPENSIVE LITTLE WIFIE?"
Jones (who has spent the morning and a small fortune at the Magasin du Louvre): "WELL, YOU ARE A LITTLE DEAR!"

Gran'pa Macpherson: "HOW MANY DOES TWO AND TWO MAKE, DONALD?"
Donald: "SIX."
Gran'pa: "WHAT ARE YE TALKING ABOUT? TWO AND TWO MAKE FOUR."
Donald: "YES, I KNOW; BUT I THOUGHT YOU'D 'BEAT ME DOWN' A BIT!"

Bill Sykes (reading): "THERE ARE NOW TEN MEN OF THE BECHUANALAND BORDER POLICE IN THE WHOLE OF BECHUANALAND PROTECTORATE, FOUR OF WHOM ARE DOING CUSTOMS DUTY."

Commissionaire: "WOULD YOU LIKE A FOUR-WHEELER OR A 'ANSOM, SIR?"
Convivial Party (indistinctly): "VER' MUSH OBLIGE—BUT—REELY DON'T THINK I *COULD* TAKE 'NY MORE!"

GLADSTONE

SALISBURY

CHAMBERLAIN

dinner. The great man was delighted because even in the 'nineties *Punch* was well known to him. Burnand greeted his honoured guest gratefully and promptly made him an honorary member of the *Punch* table, a distinction shared later by James Thurber and the Duke of Edinburgh.

Mark Twain returned to the States in 1899, no doubt with happy memories of abundant hospitality and English goodwill because he returned in the summer of the following year. He attended an evening at the Savage with J. Macalister in the chair: Phil May draw an impromptu sketch of the occasion, placing himself in the mêlée. The following month Mark Twain himself accepted an evening in the chair and, as Aaron Watson recalled, "It was the biggest and most jovial dinner of the year, with Mark Twain diffusing around him an atmosphere of high exhilaration." It was against the rules to make speeches but, as he was in the chair, Twain intended to make as many speeches as he liked; and he did, with great wit and raillery.

Romano's, the National Sporting Club, the old Gaiety Bar and, of course, the Savage together formed the mainstay of Phil May's life in the 'nineties. These were his chief ports of refuge, though the incorrigible man about town could wander into any bar in London with the aura of a pop star. He was equally popular with the cabbies, and in particular with his own "regular". One night, after his weekly *Punch* dinner, Phil's cabbie Gilbert, far from sober himself, drove him home in a normal inebriated state. When the cab reached Rowsley House it stopped, giving Phil plenty of time to alight before Gilbert drove solemnly back to the depôt at Kensal Rise. The next morning at daybreak, as Phil was sleeping peacefully in the cab, he was suddenly awakened by a strong jet of cold water. The cab-washer was even more surprised than Phil when a head appeared from the depths of the hansom. "Cor, I'm blowed if it ain't Gilbert's regula'!" he exclaimed to a disgruntled May.

On another occasion when Phil could not remember much — and, in particular, not the name and address of a friend he wished to visit, he drew a sketch for Gilbert. "It's neerachurch," he slurred, and Gilbert was able to recognise his destination. He was able to take Phil May there and furthermore, realising the value of the sketch, quickly pocketed it.

Phil's familiarity with his cabbies was extended also to his models, his favourite among whom was George Riches, who frequently modelled for the Langham Sketch Club. Riches, a cockney of the old school who lived in Kilburn, is best remembered for his Georgian get-up, but he had a vast array of costumes and he could adapt himself to any character, from lord to loafer, or, in May's phrase, "anything from rakes to monks". He appears in May's work in many guises; on one occasion he even posed as an old woman. Riches was something of a character. When he sat for May he would help himself liberally to the ever-open bottle. Some years later, when posing for another less generous artist, he came off badly when helping himself to an inviting bottle.

> He tossed off most of the drink, and then there was a violent outburst of spluttering and oaths. The bottle was a dummy for use in window-dressing and the contents smelt all too strongly of eggs long unfit for human consumption.

10 A Fellow of Infinite Jest

I N 1902 the Mays once again moved. This time they chose St John's Wood, and settled into 5 Melina Place, off Grove End Road.

By this time Phil's face was badly disfigured through drinking; Lilian tried to hide her anxiety as his drinking bouts continued unabated, but eventually he lost so much weight and the doctor's warnings had become so adamant, that she put her foot down. He was not to go out unaccompanied.

One frequent visitor to Melina Place during the latter part of his life was the portrait painter J. J. Shannon. He was one of May's greatest admirers and the excellent portrait which Shannon did of him, which now hangs in the Tate Gallery, captures May exactly. "A perfect masterpiece, my boy," Phil described it, "he hasn't missed a single ... pimple!" Shannon had also painted the portrait of Sir Thomas Dewar of Dewar's whisky and Phil suggested that the two portraits be hung side by side at the Royal Academy, with the caption "Cause and Effect".

James Jebusa Shannon (1862-1923) has been considered by some a rival to Sargent and it is surprising that no biography of this American-born genius has yet been published. Elected to the Royal Academy and eventually knighted, Shannon looked every inch the great portrait painter, while his paintings sparkle with vitality and preserve the essence of the late Victorian and Edwardian period.

Shannon tactfully diagnosed Phil's facial disfigurement as erysipelas, a skin disorder, but his polite disguising of the truth was soon rumbled. Naturally May was sensitive about his appearance and became uncertain of pushing himself into company. One evening when he went to visit Shannon he was surprised to find a party in progress. Not wishing to join in the fun, he insisted on remaining in the billiard room. Shannon joined him there as Phil amused himself by rolling empty tumblers into the pockets of the billiard table. News of his arrival soon reached the other guests, however, who one by one drifted to the billiard room until the whole party surrounded him.

Lilian stuck close by Phil through the terrible time when his body began reacting against the constant poisoning by whisky and cigars. Even in extremities, Phil always spoke and thought of her affectionately. After an evening out, not characterised by abstinence, Phil was being accompanied home from the Savage Club — as directed by Lilian — by a friend, when their hansom passed Covent Garden flower market at its busiest hour of 4 a.m. "Roses!" Phil exclaimed, "red roses! Lil loves them!" At once he had the cab filled with red roses till it could hold no more. Arriving home, he found, as he usually did, that Lilian was asleep. Without waking her, he piled roses all round her on the bed, slept on the sofa, and left her to wake in the morning bowered and covered with her favourite flowers.

On a similar occasion, however, a truant night's idyllic ending was turned into burlesque. It was not so late in the morning, though the circumstances were otherwise much the same; perhaps Phil was somewhat drunker. It was past midnight and Covent Garden market was deserted. A determined friend had planted Phil in a hansom; "Straight home!" was the order. But Phil was insistent

Phil May, by Sir J. J. Shannon
(Courtesy of the Tate Gallery)

113

on taking back some small peace-offering "for the Missus". Flowers were out of the question, and so, it seemed to his friend, was everything else. But Phil knew better. "There's a fishmonger's in Park Road," he said, "stop there," and immediately fell asleep. But not for long. As though by instinct he roused himself at Park Road, looked out, and stopped the cab at the desired spot. The shop, of course, was in darkness, but the unabashed Phil stumbled out of the cab, rang the bell, and attacked the door with both fists, calling to the slumbering tradesman to come down. Presently a window opened above and a sleepy head appeared.

"Is that Mr May?" asked the fishmonger.

"Yes — come down! I want something for Mrs May. Got a lobster?"

"No, there's nothing, Mr May; it's hot weather, and I've cleared off everything. The shop's empty. Good night!"

"Goodnight be blowed!" retorted May, redoubling his assault on the door. "Come down! Got a fowl? Pair o' ducks? Bit o' salmon? Must have *something*!"

"There's nothing at all, Mr May!" pleaded the shopkeeper. "Nothing 'til morning," and he closed the window.

"Well it *is* morning. Come on! Must have something! What sort o' shop's this? Got nothing!" More thumps on the door.

There was nothing else for it; the unhappy tradesman descended the stairs, unbolted the door, turned on the light and displayed the empty shop. "Look for yourself, sir — there's not a thing! If you won't believe me, look!"

But May's eagle eye noticed something in a far corner. "What's that?" he demanded, advancing into the shop and pointing.

"That? That's a conger eel! You don't want a conger eel for Mrs May! There's nothing else, nothing whatever!"

Phil stood over the conger eel — an enormous five-foot specimen; then, with a last glance round the empty shop, he fell on the slimy dead monster with both hands. "All right! Got nothing else — this'll have to do. Must have something!"

The fishmonger, who was dying to get back to bed, gave Phil some wrapping paper, and May and his sea-serpent blundered back to the hansom. But the paper was inadequate and the slippery creature escaped in all directions. As his companion observed afterwards, the situation in the cab during the progress to Melina Place closely resembled a grapple with the Loch Ness Monster.

Poor Lilian had her "little surprise". With a vague recollection of his success with the roses, Phil triumphantly dumped the slithering horror on the bed, which woke her with a start to confront the ophidian nightmare that surpassed her wildest dreams. "It must have been a bit of a shock," May confessed in more sober moments, "but she stood it, dear old Missus — stood it like a brick, till she began sorting out the beastly wrapping papers and found among them the drawings that I ought to have left at the *Graphic* office!"

Thomas J. Barratt, in *The Annals of Hampstead*, has a good story of May: "I found him one morning in his armchair in a studio he temporarily occupied at Haverstock Hill, which chair had evidently been his resting-place for part of the night. He said he had been awakened there by a burglar who had entered the studio and who, immediately on discovering Phil, tried to decamp. The latter, however, invited him to take a chair by the fire with him and enjoy some whisky and cigars. He told me he had just let the burglar out when I came in. Knowing his nature as I did, I quite believe the tale was true."

May visited the Royal Academy for the first time in 1902, when he saw his own portrait painted by Shannon, the finest work in that summer exhibition. His only

"PENNY 'ADDICK."
"FINNEN?"
"NO; THICK 'UN!"

"PLEASE, SIR, TUPPENCE WORTH OF BUTTER SCRAPIN'S,
AN' MOTHER SAYS BE SURE THEY'RE ALL *CLEAN*,
'CAUSE SHE'S EXPECTIN' COMPANY."

Youngster (who has just had a penny given to him):
"'OW MUCH IS THEM GRAPES, MISTER?"
Shopkeeper (amused): "THEY ARE FOUR SHILLINGS AND
SIXPENCE A POUND, MY LAD."
Youngster: "WELL, THEN, GIVE US A 'A'PORTH O' *CARROTS*.
I'M A *DEMON* FOR *FRUIT!*"

"WELL, THERE'S YOUR TREACLE. NOW WHERE'S YOUR
TWOPENCE?"
"MOTHER PUT IT IN TH' JUG!"

contribution to the Academy had been his drawings for J. M. Barrie's *The Little Minister*, exhibited in 1898. Lilian once remarked that, "Phil never goes to picture galleries — that is, if you except those in Holland, where he always has a look round." One of Phil's prize possessions was in fact a book on Frans Hals with some splendid reproductions. When paging through these one day, he stopped, looked for a long time, and then, turning in a kind of ecstasy, said, "Can't the beggar draw hands!"

Phil's escapades were meantime becoming more erratic and a number of fellow Savage Club members noticed his rapid deterioration. Even that old bounder E. J. Odell took pity on his former tormentor and, at two o'clock one morning when Phil lay in a stupor in one of the comfortable leather armchairs, having drunk his guard under the table before midnight, Odell deputised for the incapacitated companion and undertook the dangerous mission of seeing Phil May home. By gentle persuasion he eventually succeeded in getting Phil to leave the club and clamber into a cab. When they arrived at Melina Place, Odell carefully took Phil's latch-key from his pocket, opened the door and deposited Phil on a couch in the hall to sleep it off. Without disturbing Mrs May he let himself out and softly closed the door behind him. Unfortunately he did not have enough cash on him to pay for a cab back to the club, so he walked all the way from St John's Wood to Adelphi Terrace. Still, he felt he had rendered a worthwhile service to an old colleague. However, when returned to the club, there was the slim figure of Phil May at the bar with a broad grin on his face and a glass held aloft.

This present state of dependence was a reversal of rôles for Phil, who had spent most of his life seeing other people home. He was exceptionally fortunate in the permissive Lilian, who understood his problems and was well-orientated to club life. One of May's drinking companions, John L. Sullivan, a prize fighter with a thick-set physique and ferocious appearance, was too scared stiff of his own wife to venture home brazenly in an inebriated state, and he could expect to be walloped if he had stopped out all night. Sullivan commandeered poor Phil, the gentlest and frailest of men, to be pushed into his house to break the glad tidings to Mrs Sullivan that John L. had come home.

After one of these nights on the town, Phil awoke feeling, surprisingly, better than he had for weeks. He was in such fine spirits that he rose before noon and went down to the old Gambrinus Tavern which used to be in Regent Street. A friend who noticed him come in was with a young girl student, and he beckoned Phil to join them. Phil sat down and merrily chirped away but, after a few minutes, the girl, who couln't keep her eyes off his enlarged, red nose, began to embarrass Phil. "Ah!" he said good naturedly, "You are looking at my nose. It is my most expensive possession; it has cost me over £30,000 to acquire it!"

Phil May was that rare type of man who left a lasting impression on people. As a friend wrote: "In spite of all his faults and weaknesses, May was a man to whom one could not help being very much attracted. He was always gentlemanly in behaviour, had charming manners, was a very good talker on many subjects, very witty, and a great lover of music. I have seen him cross-grained, very, very depressed, and out of temper, but his charming manner never deserted him."

Once May sold a sketch to an American collector for £50 and decided to buy himself a fur-lined coat from the proceeds. After showing it to Lilian, who approved his purchase, he went to the Savage Club and spent the entire evening wearing it at the bar. Proudly displaying his new acquisition to everyone and insisting that they admire it, he suggested that other members should buy one like it. "Wearing one of

East End Loafers
(From "The Century Magazine")

these makes me look like a ruddy Australian millionaire!" he barked, and proceeded to prance about like a debutante exhibiting a new gown. It was a beautiful coat, with a collar and cuffs of astrakhan, and lined with sleek fur.

The weather was bitterly cold and snow was falling when Phil left the club. He tried to find a hansom but the streets were empty, so he decided to walk home. On the way he came upon a vagrant huddled on a park bench, fast asleep but shivering as the snow softly covered him. Mindful of his own park-bench days, Phil stripped off his new coat and covered the tramp.

This was not the last Phil was to hear of his coat: the repercussions of his act of good-Samaritanism were to reach the press the following day. Much to Phil's embarrassment, a policeman had apprehended the tramp and asked how he had come by such a very expensive coat. As the unfortunate man could offer no explanation, he was marched off to the police station where letters addressed to Phil May, Esquire, The Savage Club, were found in his coat pockets. As a result, Phil was forced to make a reluctant appearance in court to clear the tramp's name.

Phil May was also frequently in trouble with his editors, and caused them frequent embarrassment. His capacity for whittling away his financial resources at the bar led him into many a ploy to earn some quick money. One of his sources of a little extra cash was the editor of the *Sketch*, John Keble Bell, better known under his pseudonym of Keble Howard. He had taken over the editorship of the *Sketch* in 1902 after the death of John Latey. He was only twenty-seven years old at the time of his first meeting with Phil, which was recorded in his autobiography, *My Motley Life*:

> I was leaving the office one evening when a man passed me with an artist's portfolio under his arm. I had never met him before but I recognised Phil May immediately and, surmising that he might want to see me in my capacity as editor of the *Sketch*, I darted back into my office by another entrance. No sooner had I sat down than there was a knock at the door and Phil May was announced.
>
> "Good evening," said May with a broad grin stretching from one side of his face to the other, "I've brought you a drawing," and he fished into his portfolio to pull out an exquisite caricature of George Robey dressed in prehistoric costume.
>
> I looked at the drawing. "Are you offering this for the *Sketch*," I asked. This may have sounded a foolish question, but I knew Phil May was on the staff of *Punch*, and *Punch* men were not, as a rule, allowed to work for any other weekly paper. Still, it was not my business to know the ins and outs of Phil May's contract, or to cross-examine him about it.
>
> "Yes, if you care to publish it," Phil said.
>
> "I should certainly like to publish it. How much?"
>
> "Oh, the old price, I suppose."
>
> "What was that?"
>
> He told me. It was the same price that I paid to all our leading artists. "But I'd like it now," he added.
>
> The cashier had not left the building, so I sent to him for the money. While we were waiting for it, I had an idea. "You're interested in Shakespeare, aren't you?" I said.
>
> "Very," was the answer.
>
> "Well, why not do me some illustrations from Shakespeare with your own special touch? I mean, take a well-known line from Shakespeare and make something funny out of it. I'll run the series and call it 'Shakespeare Illustrated by Phil May'." He jumped at it. For one thing, it saved him the trouble of inventing a new punch line each week — the greatest bugbear to all humorous artists. Apart from which the idea was a good one.
>
> He went off with his money, being met at the top of Milford Lane by a nice little group of friends, and in due course we started our series.

"THERE'S ONE THING I *WILL* SAY ABOUT ME — AN' THAT IS, I'S A MAN OF REGULAR 'ABITS!"

SO LIKELY!

SCENE — *Bar of a Railway Refreshment Room*
Barmaid: "TEA, SIR?"   Mr Boozy: "TEA!!! ME!!!!"

MAFEKING NIGHT

(*Or rather* 3 A.M. *the following morning*)
Voice (*from above*): "GOOD GRACIOUS, WILLIAM! WHY *DON'T* YOU COME TO BED?"
William (*huskily*): "MY DEAR MARIA, YOU KNOW IT'S BEEN THE RULE OF MY LIFE TO GO TO BED SHOBER — AND I CAN'T POSH'BLY COME TO BED YET!"

CHRISTMAS COMES BUT ONCE A YEAR

Cabby (*to Gent who has been dining out*): "'ERE Y'ARE SIR. THIS IS YOUR 'OUSE — GET OUT — BE CAREFUL, SIR, 'ERE'S THE STEP."
Gent: "YESH! THASH ALLRI', BUT WERSH MY *FEET*?"

SHAKESPEARE ILLUSTRATED
"I AM DOWN AGAIN!" — *Cymbeline*, Act V, Sc. 5

When it had been running merrily for a few weeks, I received a letter from Sir Francis Burnand of *Punch*, in which he pointed out that nobody wished to injure dear old Phil May, but that his contract with *Punch* prohibited his working for any other weekly paper. He went on to say that his firm would gladly take over any drawings we had in stock, at the price that we had paid for them, and any blocks that had already been made. There was nothing for it but to surrender the drawings and the blocks, and for Phil's sake my series was transferred to the pages of *Punch*.

Towards the end of 1902 Phil May was drinking three or four bottles of Scotch a day. The more he drank, the more he needed, and there were times when he was

Study for the finished drawing

FOGGY WEATHER

"Has Mr Smith been here?"
"Yes; he was here about an hour ago."
"Was I with him?"

totally unaware of his surroundings. Already the previous year, on the day of Queen Victoria's funeral, he dressed up in his usual loud riding clothes of check lustre and went down to the Savage Club, unaware that everyone else was wearing black until Raven-Hill reminded him what day it was. "I clean forgot!" explained Phil apologetically. "But here I am, and I can't do anything about it now — unless I put burnt cork on my nose!"

Raven-Hill, the Bath-born cartoonist who had worked beside Phil May on the magazine *Pick-Me-Up*, had recently been elected to the *Punch* table. This chubby, jovial humourist was one of Phil's most loyal admirers and friends, and like the others he sadly watched Phil's failing health and realised nothing could be done to change his erratic behaviour. One day Phil May appeared at the Savage Club with the most enormous cigar ever seen. "Good heavens, Phil!" exclaimed Raven-Hill. "Where did you get that thing?"

"Had it made," was Phil's placid reply. "Had to wait months for 'em. You see, the doctor cut me down to seven cigars a day!"

In an attempt to recuperate from his bouts of dissipation, Phil May, with Lilian's approval, visited the village of Broadway in Gloucestershire for a short holiday. Needless to say, he spent much time propped up at the bar of the Lygon Arms, continuing his alcoholic decline. Nevertheless, he did manage to complete a few sketches of local characters and two finished drawings for *Punch*. One delightful reminder of his stay was a picture postcard of the entrance to the Lygon Arms on which he drew a truthful self-caricature, showing himself looking thin, haggard and old, but still with the inevitable smile. This postcard and both *Punch* drawings can today be seen in a charming little cubby-hole to the right as you enter the Lygon Arms.

Phil himself was all too conscious of what he was suffering at the hands of his endless cigars and the dreaded "alc". His over-indulgence over many years, coupled with over-work and playing too hard combined to create the tragedy of his life. As early as 1897 he had written to a friend, "I have been very unwell and over-worked for the last year or more, and it is beginning to tell on me. I don't see any prospect of a rest." Lilian and his doctor struggled in vain to help him but his enormous circle of friends and hangers-on absorbed too much of his life. His pace and the hopeless irregularity of his habits produced the inevitable result.

As Phil lay on his deathbed he faced the end with a smile. "These doctors," he told Shannon, "are very difficult. I've been told to take exercise for my liver and to stop in bed for my lungs!". He died on August 5th 1903 with Lilian at his bedside. As he drifted away his skin seemed to take on a translucent quality which hid the blemishes and the corrugations of strain.

Francis Burnand had persuaded him to convert to Roman Catholicism just before his death, and accordingly he was buried in St Mary's Roman Catholic Cemetery at Kensal Rise. "Pray for the soul of Philip William May", his gravestone proclaimed. He weighed only five stone when he died. His finances he left in an inextricable tangle. Some weeks before, seeing what was to come, he had told Lilian, "If anything happens to me, I want you to re-marry."

"What are you talking about?" Lilian had replied, though she well knew how ill he was.

"How about John Ross, he's a decent bloke. I've made a right mess of things and you deserve someone better." Lilian had burst into tears, though much later those words came back.

Meanwhile, on Lilian's behalf, "Phil May's Widow Fund" was started and a

SO VERY CONSIDERATE

Stout Coster: "WHERE ARE YER GOIN' TO, BILL?"

Bill: "INTER THE COUNTRY FOR A NICE DRIVE, BEIN' BANK 'OLIDAY."

Stout Coster: "SAME 'ERE. I SY! DON'T YER THINK WE MIGHT SWOP MISSESES JUST FOR A FEW HOURS? IT WOULD BE SO MUCH KINDER TO THE *HANIMILE*?"

AN INFORMAL INTRODUCTION

'Arry (shouting across the street to his pal): "HI! BILL! THIS IS 'ER!"

Loafer: "ANY CHANCE OF A JOB O' WORK 'ERE, MISTER?"

Foreman: "NO. WE'RE NOT WANTING ANY MORE HANDS NOW."

Loafer: "WELL, THE LITTLE BIT OF WORK *I'D* DO WOULDN'T MAKE NO DIFFERENCE!"

First Workman: "WHY DON'T YER BUY YER *OWN* MATCHES, 'STEAD OF ALWAYS CADGIN' MINE?"

Second Workman: "YOU'RE UNCOMMON MEAN WITH YER MATCHES. I'LL JUST TAKE A FEW" — *(helps himself to two-thirds)* — "AND BE HINDERPENDENT OF YER!"

The Vicar: "I'M SURPRISED AT *YOU* MIGGS. WHY, LOOK
AT *ME.* I CAN GO INTO THE TOWN WITHOUT COMING·
BACK INTOXICATED."
Miggs: "YESH, ZUR, BUT *OI* BE SO POPULAR!" (*Hic*)

Old Lady (describing a cycling accident): "'E 'ELPED
ME HUP, AN' BRUSHED THE DUST ORF ON ME, AN' PUT
FIVE SHILLIN' IN MY 'AN SO I SAYS, 'WELL, SIR, I'M SURE
YOU'RE *HACTIN*' LIKE A GENTLEMAN,' I SAYS, 'THOUGH
I DON'T SUPPOSE YOU ARE ONE,' I SAYS."

The Vicar: "I HAVE NOT SEEN YOUR HUSBAND AT CHURCH
LATELY, MRS MURPHY."
Mrs Murphy: "WELL, SIR, I'M SORRY TO SAY AS MY OLD
MAN IS *ENJOYING* VERY BAD 'EALTH AT PRESENT!"

Serious Old Party: "EH, BUT THIS IS A WICKED WORLD!"
Flippant Individual: "YOU ARE RIGHT, MRS MUMBLE.
FOR MY PART, I SHALL BE QUITE SATISFIED IF I GET
OUT OF IT ALIVE!"

letter circulated which began, "As you will know, Phil May was careless in money matters and often imposed upon . . . as a result Mrs May is left with no property of her own." The list of the Widow Fund's Committee included Sir William Agnew, Sir Edward Poynter and Sir John Tenniel, while among the contributors were Bernard Partridge, L. Raven-Hill and J. J. Shannon.

Lilian did indeed marry John Ross, that stalwart member of the National Sporting Club and Kennel Club, though the marriage was to be short-lived, Lilian herself dying in 1909, less than six years after Phil. In that same year a committee was formed in Leeds for the erection of a plaque on the house in which Phil May had been born. Caldwell Spruce sculpted a bronze portrait medallion which was set in a piece of marble and erected on the wall of 66 Wallace Street. The caricaturist E. T. Reed was invited to unveil the plaque and a number of Phil May's *Punch* colleagues attended the ceremony, including Sir Henry Lucy, who remarked: "While one is inclined to respect Charles Keene, one has to love Phil May. With all his faults, he was too good a fellow to go anywhere but Heaven, although it will be a disappointment to the other place. The first thing he would have done was to stand drinks all round."

In its day 66 Wallace Street was visited by many hundreds of admirers who negotiated the potholes and cobwebs to view the famous frontage. The occupants had the distinction of being known as "t' people wi't plaque". However, in 1965 Phil May's birthplace was pulled down to make way for an old people's home called Phil May Court. The last person to occupy number 66 was, fittingly, the tenant of an off-licence. The plaque which marked the house has been preserved by the Leeds City Art Gallery. It is fitting that in 1976 the Greater London Council decided to honour Phil May with a blue plaque on Rowsley House at 20 Holland Park Road, where he and Lilian had lived between 1896 and 1899.

Phil May had been the instinctive artist right up until the very end. A collection of sketches was even discovered under his bed after his death. One depicts a skeleton with Death hovering over him and dancing skeletons garlanded with roses beckoning him to join them. In lighter vein, a few days earlier he had written his own epitaph:

> Here lies poor old Phil.
> While he lived he lied his fill,
> And, now he's dead,
> He's lying still.

"The Upper Ten"

"Sweet Violets"

'Arriet

Epilogue

Phil May had burnt the candle at both ends for far too long, but although his untimely death closed a chapter in graphic art history, the work he left behind him opened another. A mélange of followers sprang up after his death. There were many admirers who mourned his tragic loss — *Punch* cartoonist Bert Thomas, John Hassall, James Thorpe, George Belcher. Thomas looked on May as an idol and even brushed his hair forward in the same style. Perhaps he went a bit too far when he asked to be buried next to May at Kensal Rise. All of these artists pledged their allegiance to the Phil May wit. Hassall was not only artistically influenced by May but also adopted his social habits, while James Thorpe devoted a large slice of his life to studying May's work, and his own cartoons look like watered-down versions of May's. George Belcher was probably the most successful imitator of May's style, expressed in the medium of charcoal.

Many other artists too were to acknowledge Phil May's genius; there were David Low and H. M. Bateman. Even today major talents such as Tidy, Larry, McMurtry, Ronald Searle, Scarfe, Michael Heath, Thelwell, Graham, Langdon, ffolkes and Honeysett have all benefited from Phil May's lessons on the simplicity of line. May's lead was so great that many artists have followed, using his technique as the basis for their own art. May's verve and dexterity with a pen were beyond reproach; his drawings can be read like a kind of handwriting, telling their own story, while on another level the autobiographical and social element is clear and honest, providing an accurate account of Phil May's life and times.

The last word must go to Charles Dana Gibson (of "Gibson Girl" fame), who said, "If a man's bad, I can tell you why he's bad: but when he's as good as Phil May, I can't tell you why he's good, because if I could I would do exactly the same."

Phil May's first
"Punch" cartoon

"AND SHE OUGHT TO KNOW"
"That's supposed to be a portograph of Lady Solsbury. But, bless yer, it ain't like her a bit in private!"

127

Select Bibliography

Allison, William, *My Kingdom for a Horse*
Armour, G. D., *Bridle and Brush*
Booth, J. B., *Sporting Times*
Bradshaw, Percy, *Brother Savages and Guests*
Bridges, T. C., *Florida to Fleet Street*
Bruce, J. F., *The Art of Blamire Young*
Cuppleditch, David, *The London Sketch Club*
Deghy, Guy, *Paradise in the Strand*
Duffield, K., *Savages and Kings*
Edwards, Lionel, *Reminiscences of a Sporting Artist*
Gribble, F., *The Phil May Folio*
Halkett, G. R., *A Phil May Picture Book*
Hambourg, M., *The Eighth Octave*
Howard Keble, *My Motley Life*
Hudson, D., *James Pryde*
Low, David, *Autobiography*
Moore, Augustus, *The Phil May Album*
Nevill, R., *Unconventional Memories and Night Life*
Pennell, E. R., *Nights*
Robey, George, *After Dinner Stories*
Rothenstein, W., *Men and Memories*
Stephens, A. G., *Phil May in Australia*
Thorpe, James, *English Illustration: The Nineties*
Thorpe, James, *Phil May: 1864-1903*
Thorpe, James, *Phil May, Master Draughtsman and Humourist*
Ward, Edwin, *Recollections of a Savage*
Watson, Aaron, *The Savage Club*